The
Mountain Hut
Book

Printed in China on behalf of Latitude Press Ltd
A catalogue record for this book is available from the British Library.
All photographs are by the author unless otherwise stated.

Route mapping by Lovell Johns www.lovelljohns.com
Contains OpenStreetMap.org data © OpenStreetMap contributors, CC-BY-SA.
NASA relief data courtesy of ESRI

Acknowledgements

My thanks as ever to Jonathan Williams at Cicerone for his initial enthusiasm to take this book on, and my apologies for keeping him guessing as to its content until the very last moment. I am grateful, too, to all the Cicerone team who put it together, especially Pat Dunn, my editor, and designer Clare Crooke. Not only are they highly skilled at what they do, but they are such lovely people to work with, and I trust they know how much I value their special friendship. Thank you, each one. My good friend Gillian Price, whose personal experience of the Dolomites is much greater than mine, generously provided a description of one of her favourite huts as well as the spectacular Alta Via 2 trek across those bewitching mountains, and gave me access to some of her splendid photographs with which to illustrate them. Thanks, Gillian, I'm in your debt! I'm also grateful to Anaïs Bobst at Switzerland Tourism for the image of the new Monte Rosa Hut. And to my wife Min and our daughters, and all those with whom I've shared unforgettable hutting experiences in various parts of the world – my love and thanks for adding to life's riches.

Mountain safety

Every mountain walk has its dangers, and those described in this guidebook are no exception. All who walk or climb in the mountains should recognise this and take responsibility for themselves and their companions along the way. The author and publisher have made every effort to ensure that the information contained in this guide was correct when it went to press, but, except for any liability that cannot be excluded by law, they cannot accept responsibility for any loss, injury or inconvenience sustained by any person using this book.

To call out the Mountain Rescue, ring 999 (in the UK) or the international emergency number 112: this will connect you via any available network. Once connected to the emergency operator, ask for the police.

Front cover: *The Mönch and Jungfrau, viewed from Schynige Platte at the start of the Tour of the Jungfrau Region*
Opposite page: *Secluded among some of the finest of all Swiss mountains, Cabane d'Arpitettaz was built in 1953 by seven Zinal guides*

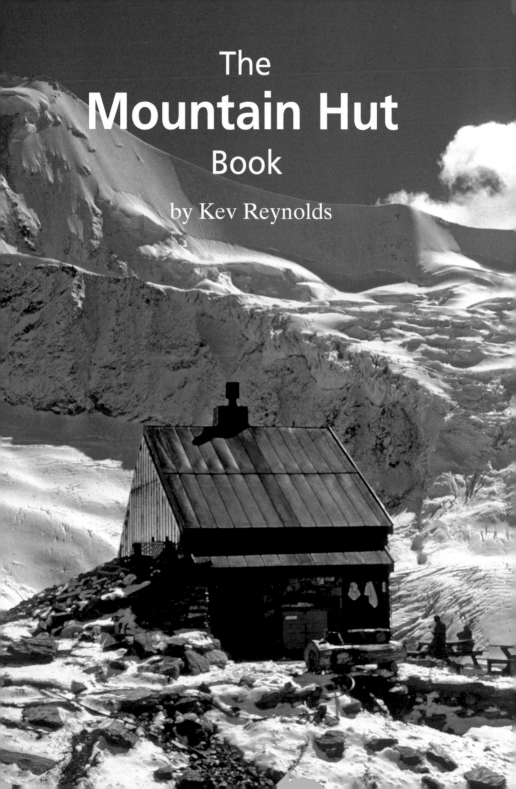

The
Mountain Hut
Book

by Kev Reynolds

Dedication

To all the hut guardians, known and unknown, whose personality and efforts add so much to the mountain experience

Refuge de la Leisse, a group of three buildings reached after crossing a col which carries the Vanoise National Park bound~

Contents

The mountain hut –
an outlook on another world

From the Col de la Chavière there are spectacular views north towards the Grande Casse and Mont Blanc on a clear day (Photo: Jonathan Williams)

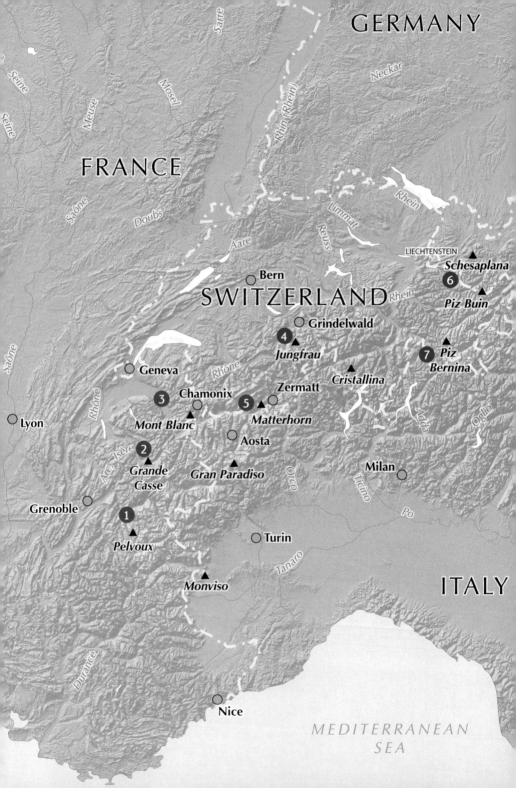

Vienna

Munich

Salzburg

9 Ellmauer Halt

Watzmann

AUSTRIA

Zugspitze

Inn

Innsbruck

Salzach

8 Hochfeiler

Zuckerhütl

Großglockner

Idspitze

Drava

10

Bolzano

Marmolada

Triglav

Trento

Piave

Ljubljanica

Sava

Ljubljana

Ljubljanica

SLOVENIA

Trieste

Venice

Kupa, Sava

Adige

Una

ADRIATIC
SEA

Reno

N

Arno

Tevere

Tibre

0   100 miles

0   200km

1	Tour of the Oisans
2	Tour of the Vanoise
3	Tour of Mont Blanc
4	Tour of the Jungfrau Region
5	Tour of the Val de Bagnes
6	Rätikon Höhenweg
7	Tour of the Bernina
8	Stubai High-Level Route
9	Tour of the Wilder Kaiser
10	Alta Via 2

Seen from Cabane de Panossière, the Grand Combin rises above the Corbassière glacier

Symbols used on route maps

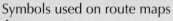 route

   alternative route

 S start point

 F finish point

SF start/finish point

 S alternative start

SF alternative start/finish point

 glacier

 woodland

town or village

international border

 station/railway

 cablecar/gondola

 ▲ peak

 ⇧ café or restaurant

 ⬆ refuge hut, *gîte* or mountain hut

⏝ pass

HUT ROUTES

SCALE: 1:50,000

TOURS

SCALE: 1:250,000

5000 and above	3200–3400	
4800–5000	3000–3200	1400–1600
4600–4800	2800–3000	1200–1400
4400–4600	2600–2800	1000–1200
4200–4400	2400–2600	800–1000
4000–4200	2200–2400	600–800
3800–4000	2000–2200	400–600
3600–3800	1800–2000	200–400
3400–3600	1600–1800	0–200

The solid-looking Brèche de Roland refuge in the Cirque de Gavarnie (French Pyrenees)

Introduction

A mountain hut is a purpose-built refuge situated at some strategically high place in the mountains so that one or more peaks are readily accessible from it. It may vary in size from a simple bivouac shelter to something resembling a small hotel in size and facilities.

This quote, taken from Walt Unsworth's *Encyclopaedia of Mountaineering* (1992), describes the original use for which huts were built, but it tells only part of the story. With the remarkable increase in outdoor activity since it was written, huts have had to evolve, and today there must be as many walkers and trekkers as there are climbers who choose to stay in them.

Over several decades of activity I've visited or stayed in hundreds of mountain huts (otherwise known as a *cabane*, *capanna* or *chamanna*, *dom* and *koča*, *Hütte*, *refuge* or *rifugio*), not just in the Alps, but also in the Pyrenees, Morocco, Russia and the high Himalaya, where they are known by other names, and I've come to appreciate the sheer variety and sometimes quirky nature of such dwellings lodged in a remote corner of the mountains far from the familiar everyday world. Here, it's possible to be alone, if I wish,

or be drawn into the babble of camaraderie to share a love of wild places with other like-minded individuals.

If you're already familiar with the hut system, you'll know that they are more than just shelters in which to pass the night – unless that's all you want of them, that is. They can be meeting places for climbers seeking a partner to tackle a particular route. They can be staging posts for trekkers on a multi-day tour. Or they can be somewhere to visit on a day's hike there-and-back from a valley base; somewhere to stop for lunch, perhaps, to sit outside in the sunshine, enjoy the view, and then move on.

During my years of guiding mountain holidays in the Alps and elsewhere, I found that clients always seemed to enjoy best the days when we visited huts, although many would openly admit to a lack of 'courage' to stay in one unless they had a friend to show them how to go about it.

Aiguille de la Tsa and the Bertol-Veisivi wall, seen from Cabane des Aiguilles Rouges

Courage seems a strange word to use in relation to something as simple as spending a night in a mountain hut, especially coming from folk who would think nothing of checking in at a three- or four-star resort hotel. But to them, huts were foreign, exotic dwellings reserved for those with experience and who were therefore assumed to hold the key to some secret world that exists among high mountains. There was an unspoken mystique about huts, secrets that only those 'in the know' were privy to. Huts were not for 'ordinary' mountain walkers.

Of course, that's nonsense!

Mountain huts are for everyone. Well, that's not strictly true, I'll admit, for some are literally out of reach, sited like some lofty eyrie inaccessible to most mountain walkers. Take, for example, the old Tour Rouge refuge in the Mont Banc massif, whose approach route was described by Hermann Buhl in *Nanga Parbat Pilgrimage* as taking him up 'a vertical, smooth crack', while the hut itself was little more than 'a prehistoric wooden shelter...consisting of three boarded walls, a corrugated iron roof and a plank floor.'

Not many 'ordinary' mountain walkers would consider tackling that route. Nor would they be likely to hanker after spending a night in such a dwelling, which is just as well, perhaps, for that quote dates from the 1950s, and the Tour Rouge refuge no longer exists.

But countless other huts do exist, and in places accessible to practically anyone who's physically active and prepared to put a bit of effort into reaching them – huts in the most remarkable places, huts with stars for neighbours, with views that remain with you for ever.

This book tells you a bit about them, shows you what and where they are, and how they have evolved from little more than the most primitive of shelters. For the uninitiated, it explains who owns them, how to use them and what facilities to expect. It shows how the hutting experience is not confined to Europe, but has spread worldwide. And it also describes a few favourite huts and a selection of hut-to-hut routes to widen your alpine horizons.

In unravelling some of the mystery, I trust this book illustrates the way in which mountain huts can be truly sociable places in which to spend a night or two in the most magical of locations, to enjoy wild nature at its very best, with spectacular views and a peace unknown in the valleys.

Why not try one, next time you're in the Alps?

1 Rooms with a view

*Amid the rude elements of nature, rock, snow and ice,
the hut is a life-giving oasis.*

(Herbert Maeder, *The Mountains of Switzerland*)

All morning the trail had gained and lost so much height that I seemed to be getting nowhere in a hurry, when at the foot of yet another steep descent the way divided, offering an escape route into the valley. Having been on the go for 5 hours and with at least another 2½ hours ahead of me (if the guardian at last night's hut at the head of Val de Bagnes was to be believed), I was almost tempted to take it – especially as close study of the map showed there were several kilometres still to cover, and more than 700m to climb in order to gain the pass whose crossing was to be the crux of the route. I felt unaccountably old and out of touch. My knees hurt and I was running short of puff. Yet 10 minutes' rest, an over-ripe banana and half a bar of chocolate put a bit of fuel in my engine, and I set off again with optimism and energy restored.

The spectacle of alpenglow on the Combin massif is one of the rewards for a night spent at the Panossière hut

Two hours later I kicked my way up a snowfield, crossed two false tops and emerged at last on the sun-dazzling crest of the Col des Otanes. The view directly ahead revealed a wonderland of ice and snow, with Combin de Corbassière rising above its glaciers, the great dome of the Grand Combin to the south, and the Dents du Midi, around which I'd trekked only a few days before, juggling wispy clouds to the north. It was a view that would have taken my breath away, if I'd had any to spare, and it made all the effort to get there worthwhile.

In no hurry now, I sat on my rucksack in the snow to savour the moment, squinting in the sunlight and soaking in the view before descending at snail's pace, content with the knowledge that before long I'd be able to relax with a cold beer in hand, the promise of a refreshing shower, a bed for the night, a three-course meal, and maybe a carafe of red wine to celebrate – not in some fancy resort hotel, but in a mountain hut set beside a glacier.

A couple of hundred metres below the col, the hut was even better than I'd hoped. Sturdy, spacious and welcoming, Cabane de Panossière stands on the right-hand lateral moraine of the Corbassière glacier in a world of its own. It has no neighbours, other than the rock, snow and ice of the mountains that drew me and the other visitors to it, and in the warmth of that bright summer's day it had everything I could possibly want or need.

Given a mattress in a room overlooking the glacier, and after satisfying a long day's mountain thirst with more over-priced cans of beer than were good for me, at 7pm that evening, along with 20 or so other climbers and walkers, I was working my way through a large plate of tender meat and spaghetti when suddenly all conversation ceased. In its place came the clatter of cutlery on china as everyone grabbed their cameras and rushed outside.

There at the head of a vast glacial highway, the Grand Combin was turning scarlet before our very eyes, its summit snows reflecting the dying sun in a riot of alpenglow, while a 1200m cascade of ice disappeared into a rising cauldron of shadow. It was one of those sights that none of us who saw it will ever forget, yet it was just one of many that the hut provided at no extra cost.

'the Grand Combin was turning scarlet before our very eyes'

Night fell not long after, leaving each one of us marooned in a world of our own – a world centred on a solitary building astride a wall of moraine among alpine giants. Peace settled; there were no alien sounds, just the occasional clunk and slither of a rock falling onto ice. It was no more threatening than the pulse beat of mountains at rest.

At 2am I slid off my bunk, tiptoed to the window and counted the stars, some of which settled on creamy summits more than 1500m above me. In the darkness, the great peaks watched over Cabane de Panossière and its guests, all of whom – except for me – were sleeping, unaware of the beauty of the scene beyond the window.

As for me, there was nowhere else I'd rather be, for my simple dormitory was the ultimate room with a view.

Huts for all

Like thousands of others scattered across the alpine chain, the Panossière Hut (www.cabane-fxb-panossiere.ch/en) provides overnight accommodation for walkers, trekkers, climbers and ski

mountaineers, and, in common with the vast majority, is located amid magnificent scenery. This one, at 2645m in the Pennine Alps of canton Valais in Switzerland, belongs to the Bourgeoisie de Bagnes, while its predecessor, destroyed by avalanche in 1988, was owned by the Swiss Alpine Club (Schweizer Alpen-Club, SAC). It can sleep 100 in its dormitories, and is manned by a guardian (or warden) during the spring ski-touring season and for about three months in the summer, when meals, drinks and snacks are available.

That, in a nutshell, sums up a modern mountain hut. It's a bit like a youth hostel, offering simple, reasonably priced

Trekking group on the trail leading to the Schesaplana Hut

accommodation and meals in a magical setting for visitors taking part in mountain activities. A 'hut' in the conventional sense it is not. There is no resemblance to a garden shed, as the word might suggest, although one of its predecessors, a simple wooden cabin built nearby in 1893, may well have been, for there were very few luxuries available in those far-off days.

A few of those early mountain refuges that gave little more than rudimentary shelter still exist today, but the majority have evolved, thank goodness, into much more comfortable buildings (the most recent claiming eco-friendly credentials, with solar generators and innovative means of water purification) that provide overnight lodging with all, or most, mod cons, three- or four-course meals and an experience to remember. Every year, thousands of mountain enthusiasts from all over the world have reason to be thankful for their existence, for they're much more than a simple home-from-home in what can sometimes be a wild and uncompromising environment. Up there, you can make contact with others who share your interests, build friendships, exchange stories and gather valuable up-to-date information about route conditions and weather forecasts from the guardians, a number of whom are also experienced mountain guides. Up there, you're in another world, divorced from everyday concerns. Up there, mountain huts become a means of escape from one reality to another, a

halfway house in which to relax during adventures 'out there'.

OK, maybe I'm nudging towards a romantic view, for it must be admitted there are those who think less favourably of the hutting experience than I. In his introduction to *100 Hikes in the Alps*, American author Harvey Edwards sets out his objections. 'They are wonderful protection in a storm,' he says, 'but I've yet to catch up on all the nights' sleep I've lost. Someone is always snoring, sneezing, singing, smoking, or getting up at 1:00am to start a climb. In season, the huts are overcrowded and often unbearable. Still, a trip to the Alps isn't worth a schnitzel if you haven't tried a hut at least once.' He then goes on to recommend using a tent.

Now I like wild camping too, and bivvying alone in remote places lost above the clouds. But there's something very special about huts, their welcome shelter and the camaraderie they inspire – especially in the *Stube* (common room/dining room) after a hard day in the hills, or (as Harvey Edwards implies) when a storm explodes outside. Any old port in a storm, you might think. Well, yes, but that's only a part of it. Having had a role to play in the history of mountaineering, they've since become an important, you might say an essential, part of the whole alpine experience – and when I say alpine, I don't just mean the European Alps (although that's the focus of this book), but any high mountain region where simple lodgings have been

After a hard day on the hill, the Stube invokes a warm sense of camaraderie as strangers who share a common enthusiasm become new-found friends

provided for those of us who are active in the great 'out there' and who, like me, look forward to spending a few nights of a holiday resting somewhere up there between heaven and earth. It's true that your sleep might be disturbed for a spell by someone snoring, but I reckon that's a small price to pay for all the rewards on offer. And you can always use ear-plugs.

I'm with Chris Bonington when he says (in *Mountaineer*): 'There is an anticipatory excitement in a crowded hut, in its babel of different languages, chance encounters with old acquaintances swilling wine and coffee, the packed communal bunks and the intensity of the early morning start.'

So where are these huts? Well, they can be found in just about every district of the 1200km alpine chain, stretching from the Maritime Alps above Nice, through France, Italy, Switzerland, Liechtenstein, Germany and Austria, to the lovely Julian and Karavanke mountains of Slovenia, and there are now so many of them that, given sufficient time, energy and ready cash, it would be possible to trek from one end of the range to the other and stay in a different hut each night. Some are grouped just an hour or so apart (there are in excess of two dozen in the Mont Blanc massif alone, a dozen on the flanks of Triglav in the

Julian Alps, and at least eight on or around the base of the Sassolungo massif in the Dolomites), while others may be spaced 5 or 6 hours – or almost a day's hike – from one another, so you can remain at high altitude for a week or more without the need to descend to a valley to find a bed for the night.

Each one will be unique – not unique in the type of sleeping accommodation on offer, since they all have some form of communal, mixed-sex dormitory, while

gourmet meals with beer or wine will be served as if in a valley hotel.

There are huts clinging to summits, huts wedged among the clefts of narrow mountain passes, huts projecting from rocky spurs secured with cables. There are huts built on moraine walls, huts in gentle meadows. Long ago there was one in the Maritime Alps that looked like a railway carriage that had been airlifted into the mountains, and there's at least one (the Rinder Hut high above

> '_There are huts clinging to summits, huts wedged among the clefts of narrow mountain passes, huts projecting from rocky spurs_'

many also have smaller two- and four-bedded rooms for greater privacy, but unique in respect of location, architectural style and ambience. Since no two huts are the same, a multi-day journey across the mountains could result in one night being spent in a converted dairy farm with 20 mattresses laid out in what used to be the milking parlour, and the next in a tiny unmanned metal cabin of a bivouac shelter anchored to a shelf of rock at 3000m with just four bunk beds, a first-aid box and a million-dollar view, while another day's hike might bring you to something better described as an almost luxurious mountain inn with room for 200 guests, decent bathroom facilities, and a cosy dining room in which

Leukerbad in Switzerland) that occupies the basement of a cable car station. When I stayed there I had the dormitory and washroom to myself, but at mealtimes was generously looked after by the Portuguese couple who'd signed up to run the cableway restaurant for the summer. They fed me as though I'd not eaten for a month, and sat me in what seemed like a great glass-domed conservatory that became a first-class observatory when darkness fell. Then they left me to enjoy the night sky and a view of snow-topped mountains stretching into the distance.

I love that diversity, the sheer variety of hut buildings and the surprise you get when you first catch sight of one

…fuge du Plan Sec is a welcome stop on the Tour of the Vanoise (Photo: Jonathan Williams)

The hut at the end of the rainbow

Cabane du Mont-Fort is one of my favourite huts. Perched high in the mountains at the western end of Switzerland's Pennine Alps, it commands one of the great alpine views, with Mont Blanc hovering far off to master-mind some of the finest sunsets you could wish to gaze on, while Daniel, the guardian who's run the place since 1983, is a cheerful host who treats all-comers as friends. It's always good to be there, and each of my visits has been memorable; only once was it memorable for the wrong reason...

It had been a long and demanding climb of more than 1600m out of the val-ley, and in the late afternoon I was growing weary when at last the path eased round the steeply sloping hillside to reveal the hut above me. But the relief that I'd always experienced when I caught sight of the familiar building with its red-striped shutters turned this time to despair.

Not more than 10 minutes' walk away, the hut looked as welcoming as ever, but the grassy slope up which my path climbed towards it was now being sprayed with liquid manure. I could smell it long before I actually saw it - the discharge from a long anaconda-like pipe that snaked across the slope and disappeared round another corner. September sunlight picked out rainbows in the pungent spray of khaki liquid that flicked in a casual arc from left to right, right to left, and back again, like some great metro-nome, ticking all the while as it washed across the hillside and covered the path - my path, and the only route to the hut.

I peered in horror at the trail ahead that was now stained with the yellow-brown liquid, and searched in vain for a way to avoid it. There was nothing obvious, so in desperation I looked for the farmer. He was nowhere to be seen, so I scanned the hillside for a dry, spray-free route to the hut, but the only one was too steep for me to contemplate and I had no appetite for that. It had taken almost 7 hours to get this far, and I was worn out.

What to do? I paced back and forth, trying to think of an alternative. How long, I wondered, would it take to get across the danger zone? Nervously I timed the arcing spray's journey from one side to the other, and doubted my ability to sprint that distance wearing a rucksack and big boots. But unless I waited until the source of the spray dried up, there was only *one thing to do. I'd just have to gamble on having enough energy to spare, take a deep breath and go for it.*

Counting the number of spray-free seconds available, I waited for the wash to pass over, then dashed up the soggy path at an Olympic pace. It was longer and steeper than I'd feared. I was slower than I'd hoped, and much too soon a shadow crossed my path and I sensed the spray's return. Relief was not more than a pace or two away, when what I'd feared came true. I slipped...

Fortunately, Cabane du Mont-Fort has decent showers, although most people take their clothes off first when using them.

you've never been to before but which is to be your home for the night. It may be a distant sighting, the flash of sunlight on a window catching your attention; or a flag on a pole beckoning from the far side of a ridge, making a useful guide in a bewildering landscape. Anticipation spurs you on. Then you top a rise, turn a corner – or the mist lifts for a moment – and there it is, journey's end at last! Arrival at the hut invariably comes with a sense of relief, for it's a guarantee of shelter, somewhere to relax, freshen up, slake your thirst and settle the nagging hunger that comes from a long day's effort.

Huts for trekkers

Manned all year round, Cabane du Mont-Fort (www.cabanemontfort.ch) is immensely popular in summer with day visitors and trekkers, while skiers flock there in winter, for access is made easy with the aid of one or more *téléphéri-*

ques (cable cars). Few trekkers' huts have such means of access, but most are approached by decent, well-marked trails and are no more than a few hours' walk apart. Facilities are usually pretty good too, enabling you to make a tour of a week or two with a backpack containing little more than a change of clothing, a sheet sleeping bag, head torch and travel towel, leaving you to enjoy the trek without being weighed down by non-essentials.

A steadily expanding network of refuges across the alpine range has enabled numerous exciting day walks and multi-day treks to be tackled by walkers of varying abilities and levels of fitness. Practically every district now claims a hut-to-hut tour that explores some of its finest scenery, encouraging newcomers to discover the mountains in all their rich variety. There are classic routes with worldwide fame, like the 10–12-day Tour

Chamanna Coaz at the head of Val Roseg in the Bernina Alps

of Mont Blanc (TMB) and the fortnight-long Walker's Haute Route from Chamonix to Zermatt (C–Z), and countless other great treks that may be less well known but are just as rewarding, with often uncrowded huts in the most amazing locations among the Alps of France, Switzerland, Austria, the Italian Dolomites and Slovenia's Julian Alps.

The Coaz Hut (Chamanna Coaz, (www.coaz.ch/en) in the Bernina Alps is a prime example. Originally built with climbers in mind, it is now regularly visited by walkers based in Pontresina or one of the nearby Engadine villages, and also by trekkers making the 9-day Tour of the Bernina. Standing close to the Roseg glacier at 2610m, some 500m above a glacial lake at the head of Val Roseg, an overnight there is a very special experience and one I'd wanted to make for many years. Despite having visited the hut several times since I first worked in the district back in the late 1960s, it wasn't until I was walking the Tour of the Bernina in 2014 that I finally had the opportunity to actually sleep there. It was early in the season and the warden was still digging a pathway through the snow when I arrived. But everything was fully operational, and as that summer happened to be the hut's 50th anniversary, anyone staying who'd been born the same year it was opened was charged at 1964 prices. Alas, I was too old for that. But at least I could claim a discount with my Alpine Club membership card.

Despite there being room for 80, I was one of only eight hikers staying (four from Sweden, two Swiss women who'd previously worked at the hut, and two of us from the UK), so there was plenty of space in the dormitories. We ate our meals together with the lights of Pontresina twinkling in the distance, to the sound of last winter's snow sliding off the roof.

On some of the more popular multi-day routes, something approaching a family atmosphere builds among trekkers, for after a few nights spent in huts and *gîtes d'étape* (walkers' hostels) along the way, you come to recognise one another, look out for a familiar face during the day, and in the evening swap stories around the dining room table. That sociability can be one of the most rewarding aspects of the hutting and trekking experience, and a number of long-lasting friendships have been created from a night shared in a mountain hut.

> 'long-lasting friendships have been created from a night shared in a mountain hut'

Take Rifugio Bonatti (www.rifugio bonatti.it) on the Tour of Mont Blanc. Named after the great Italian mountaineer Walter Bonatti, it stands on a sloping pasture on the south side of the Italian Val Ferret, with a direct view of Mont Blanc in the west and the Grandes Jorasses almost within spitting distance across the valley. Built in 1998 and privately owned, it can sleep 85 in dormitories and family-sized rooms decorated with Bonatti's photographs, and is known for the excellent facilities that make it one of the most popular huts on the tour. What's more, one of the best routes of approach (via the Mont de la Saxe option) is downhill – something of a rarity in the Alps.

The dining room is light and spacious, with big windows that exploit a wonderful panoramic view taking in much that you'll have gazed on during your hike to get there. A few years ago, my wife Min and I spent a night at the *rifugio*, as we often do, when checking the route and accommodation facilities for a new edition of my *Tour of Mont Blanc* guidebook. When the

Overlooking a tiny lake, the shingle-walled Bremer Hut belongs to the Bremen Section of the German Alpine Club

guardian sat us down for dinner that evening, we found ourselves at a table with trekkers from Australia, New Zealand, Canada, the US, South Africa and the UK, most of whom we'd been leap-frogging along the trail over the previous 5–6 days, egging each other on with cheerful comments. Now I noticed that several of them had copies of my book held open, and were discussing both the day's route and my descriptions of it. They had no idea that the author, who preferred to remain anonymous, was sitting among them, but we enjoyed the light-hearted banter that crossed international boundaries, and shared a common experience not only of the route, but of our communal home for the night. Years later, we still have regular contact with one of those trekkers from the States, exchanging trail tales via letter and email, after he'd discovered my name by accident a few days after we'd left Bonatti.

On another occasion we were working our way round Austria's lovely Stubai Alps when we spent a night at the Bremer Hut (www.bremerhuette. at). Midway through our meal, the hut warden relayed a message he'd just received by telephone from Wales, to say that one of our fellow trekkers had that very day become a grandfather for the first time. A bottle of schnapps appeared at the table, and we all drank a toast to 'granddad'! After that it was party time.

What to pack for hutting

I once led a two-centre walking holiday in the Alps, staying in hotels in each centre, but linking them with a short hut-to-hut trek. On every walk, one of the clients carried a huge backpack as though he was on a three-month Himalayan expedition. Nine-tenths of his load was included *just in case*. And nine-tenths of his load returned home with him unused. On a fortnight's trek in the Alps, staying in manned huts overnight, anything more than essentials will be unnecessary overload. A small, lightweight pack leaves the trekker free to enjoy the experience without stress or strain.

Manned huts

Here's a suggestion of what to take when using manned huts in summer:

- trekking poles
- lightweight waterproof jacket and overtrousers
- fleece jacket/sweater
- complete change of clothes
- sheet sleeping bag
- head torch
- lightweight towel
- minimum toiletries
- sunscreen
- water bottle

- map and compass
- first-aid kit
- mobile phone

Unmanned huts

In more remote districts, where huts may not be manned, all the above will be needed, plus:

- sleeping bag
- camping stove, fuel and lighter
- spork (all-in-one knife, fork and spoon)

- mug
- food
- candles
- toilet paper

A number of unmanned alpine huts have cooking facilities, crockery and cutlery – but by no means all of them. Expect nothing but shelter and a few bunk beds in remote bivvy huts. If you plan to use unmanned huts in winter, you're in a different ball game.

Huts for climbers

Huts used almost exclusively by climbers are often more spartan and less comfortable than those on major trekking routes, and some of their approaches can be long, extremely steep and sometimes hazardous. Burdened with rucksacks full of equipment, it's no wonder that climbers often consider getting to their chosen overnight base as a necessary grind to be suffered rather than enjoyed.

This is particularly true of older huts erected for the alpine pioneers, especially some of those placed in remote and seemingly inaccessible locations. For example, in 1884, in a lofty position on the graceful and isolated Monte Disgrazia in the Bregaglia Alps, Italian cartographers erected a small hut, Capanna Maria, which they presented to the Italian Alpine Club (Club Alpino Italiano, CAI). Two years later, it was visited by the Engadine

guide Christian Klucker, who described it in his autobiography *Adventures of an Alpine Guide* as 'a simple wooden shed measuring about ten feet in length, and a little more than six feet in width. A small bench, capable of seating four persons, had been fixed at the side towards the mountain. The inventory consisted of: 4 blankets, 1 small spirit-cooker with saucepan, 4 cups, and a few soup-spoons.' Of the four blankets, two were dry and fit for use, while the others were frozen to the bench. Speculating how long it would last, he was not surprised to find that by 1888 wind and storm had reduced the hut to ruins.

That was an extreme case, but access was the key. Huts built in the valleys or on lower slopes that were accessible to walkers and mountaineers of modest ambition were understandably of a much higher standard than those lodged in more challenging locations. Up there, far from roads or tracks, until comparatively recently, huts provided by the Alpine Clubs were still little more than basic lodgings, patronised by men and women with cracked and blistered skin who carried ropes, slept on communal mattresses, and rose long before dawn.

One of those women was Dorothy Pilley, who came to the Mont Blanc range in 1920 and had her first experience of a real mountain hut when she arrived at the Couvercle (https://refugeducouvercle.jimdo.com), which she found to be crowded in every corner. 'I had never seen so many tramp-like figures of all nationalities – ragged, dirty and unshaven – as were lolling about the platform, smoking and gossiping, when we trudged up the wooden steps towards them.'

Describing what she found there in her classic memoir, *Climbing Days*, she wrote: 'Through the crowd I penetrated into the dark interior of what was evidently an eating- and sleeping-room in one...A partition split off a space at one end the size of a small bathroom. This was the hut *gardien*'s sanctum, but so great was the crowd that, for a consideration, he had turned it over to the only two other women there, and suggested that I should arrange with them to share it...Seeing that the men were sleeping that night on their sides on the floor of the main room, and even some had to sleep outside in great cold, I thought myself very lucky.'

Despite this unpromising introduction, the Couvercle experience did nothing to put her off, and she came to develop a taste for hut life, describing it as 'that queer existence in between the luxuries of low, well-found camping and the high bivouacs of the pioneers.' She went on to explain to the uninitiated that there would be a pail with which to collect water from a spring or, one drop at a time, from the recesses of a crevasse. And she described eating by the light of a candle off a bare table stained with use; and sleeping side by side on mattresses stuffed with straw. Lest such privation should put her readers off, she conjured up the romance of those 'golden hours when, thousands of feet above the rest of the world, you can look out at evening from your nest upon mountains that then seem peculiarly your own.' It was for moments like these that men and women were prepared to accept the privations of a night or two marooned above the clouds.

The modern Gleckstein Hut (www.gleckstein.ch) is a far cry from the short-lived Capanna Maria on the Disgrazia, or the old Couvercle refuge with its magnificent views in the heart of the Mont Blanc range. Serving climbers tackling the Wetterhorn above Grindelwald, the Gleckstein Hut not only claims a spectacular location high above a glacier gorge at 2317m, but is surprisingly roomy and with decent facilities that include showers and four-course evening meals. Despite its location and the

Originally built as a hotel, the Gleckstein Hut in Switzerland has a fine view of the Schreckhorn

exposed nature of its approach, it is a large building with 80 places, originally built in 1904 as a hotel. At the time, there were ambitious plans to create a four-stage passenger cableway to the summit of the Wetterhorn, and one of the intermediate stations was to have been built close to where the hut stands today. But with the outbreak of World War I, the enterprise was abandoned and with few visitors the hotel closed in 1916. Four years later it was taken over by the Burgdorf section of the SAC to serve as the Gleckstein Hut.

Although its original aim was to provide accommodation for climbers, like so many other alpine huts the Gleckstein has become a popular destination for adventurous walkers and is suggested as an optional there-and-back stage for trekkers tackling the Tour of the Jungfrau Region. One of the reasons for this popularity – apart from the attraction of the hut itself – is the comparatively short (3-hour) but spectacular approach walk, which cuts along the precipitous wall of the Upper Grindelwald glacier's gorge. Narrow and exposed in places, it is safeguarded by fixed cables, at one point passes beneath a waterfall, and has exciting views throughout. On one of my visits, I sat on a rock halfway along the gorge wall and listened to the sounds of an alpenhorn echoing from one side of the valley to the other. The following morning, I opened the hut door to find half a dozen ibex licking salt from the balcony wall.

Huts for watching wildlife

A tough 5-hour climb to reach a remote hut for a sighting of a solitary ibex (see 'Where ibex roam') may be a bit extreme, but I've also studied from close quarters a dozen or more of these stocky yet incredibly agile creatures in the autumn rut just below the summit of Piz Languard. This walkers' mountain high above Pontresina is served by the simple 24-bed Georgy Hut (www.georgy-huette.ch), lodged near the top at 3202m, with an extensive panoramic view dominated by the snowy giants of Piz Palü and Piz Bernina across the valley.

Despite having a reasonable path right to the summit, Piz Languard still involves a steep ascent of over 1450m, so it's good to know that not far from here a comparatively easy 3½-hour walk goes from the Engadine village of Zernez to the log-cab-

> 'Gleckstein has become a popular destination for adventurous walkers'

in-like Chamanna Cluozza (www.nationalpark.ch) in the heart of the Swiss National Park, with virtually guaranteed views of red and roe deer, chamois, marmot and ibex along the way. A walk of similar length from Cogne – some of it on an old mule track in Italy's Gran Paradiso National Park – leads to Rifugio Vittorio Sella (www.rifugiosella.com), one of the best places

The warden at the Gleckstein Hut spreads salt on the terrace wall to attract ibex in the early morning

in all the Alps from which to study wildlife in comfort. Of an evening, scores of ibex and chamois may be seen grazing near the converted stables that make up this 150-bed hut, used by trekkers following the Gran Paradiso Alta Via 2 (not to be confused with the Dolomites Alta Via 2). Meanwhile, across the border in the Vanoise National Park in France, ibex, chamois and marmots can often be spied around the Col de la Vanoise and from several of the refuges that border the Doron gorge above Termignon – especially Refuge de l'Arpont (www. refuges-vanoise.com), a national-park-owned building renovated in 2013, which looks towards a series of waterfalls pouring over cliffs below the Vanoise glaciers.

At the head of the gorge on the eastern side of the valley, and nestling on rough pasture below the 3855m Grande Casse, the privately owned Refuge Entre Deux Eaux (www.refuge entredeuxeaux.com) is another old farm used as a refuge by trekkers following the ultra-long distance GR5, and by others straying from the splendid Tour of the Vanoise. Although not as promising for watching wildlife as Arpont, Entre Deux Eaux would be hard to beat so far as atmosphere is concerned. It is a charming, 100-year-old building, comfortably quirky and with an aura of peace that makes it a perfect haven in which to relax for a day or two.

Where ibex roam

Ibex (bouquetin in French, Steinbock in German) can often be seen grazing near huts. The wonderful Rottal Hut is one such hut, but being set 1800m above the Lauterbrunnen Valley, it's quite a haul simply to watch wildlife, although the hut and its literally breathtaking location make all the effort to get there worthwhile.

I was in the area one summer on a writing assignment with a small group making a tour of the Bernese Alps. Although a day's rest was on the itinerary when we arrived in the Lauterbrunnen Valley, I knew that a route to the Rottal Hut began not far from Stechelberg. With a reputation for having a spectacular location, the hut was, until then, one I'd only read about but longed to visit. I figured that if I could get an early lift to the roadhead, there was the possibility of making a quick there-and-back visit. Well, with more than 1800m of height to gain, the ascent might not be all that quick, but I'd give it a go, and I'd be travelling light with only the bare necessities in a small rucksack. I was also considerably younger than I am now, and fit and agile as an ibex.

So shortly after dawn next morning, I and two others left the campsite while everyone else was sleeping, and headed upvalley to the roadhead. From there, a riverside path teased us away from the village, but the gentle nature of the trail didn't last long, and within minutes of setting out, we were racing one another up a steep grassy slope before making a rising traverse to reach an alpine farmer's stone hut some 600m above the river. That left 1200m still to climb, but the views were growing with every step.

Now we cut left to enter a broad gully rising wedge-like at its head, which eventually took us to a band of abrupt, near-vertical crags split by a much tighter gully. This we climbed with the aid of fixed ropes and chains, and emerged to find a clear path winding up an old moraine rib. It continued along the crest of the moraine that flanked the Rottal glacier, then up a steep snow slope headed by a small cliff. Another fixed rope aided the ascent of these rocks, and less than 5 hours after leaving Stechelberg, we arrived at the Rottal Hut, where the first of several huge flasks of tea was soon placed before us by the part-time warden who was there just for the weekend.

At an altitude of 2755m, the Rottal Hut is very much a climbers' hut used for tackling routes on the Jungfrau, Ebnefluh and Gletscherhorn. With 34 places, it's only manned at weekends in summer, although with self-catering facilities and a wood-burning stove it's open for use at other times.

But on this occasion we were not there to climb, to stay the night or even to prepare a meal. Just being there to soak in its atmosphere was reward enough. Beyond that, we had no need to consider anything except a long knee-wrecking descent back to the valley, and a weary return to the campsite. But not yet. That would have to wait until we'd allowed time to appreciate the hut's extraordinary position under the south-west flank of the Jungfrau, and its outlook towards the head of the valley where the Lauterbrunnen Breithorn, Tschingelhorn, Blümlisalp and Gspaltenhorn rose above cascades of ice. It was a fabulous view, and I deeply regretted not being able to spend the rest of the day and a night there to soak it all in.

As if to add to the hut's appeal, as we sat outside without need for words, an ibex came clambering over rocks bordering the glacier to inspect the new arrivals.

Huts for walkers

Hundreds – perhaps thousands – of alpine huts exist that would meet the needs of mountain walkers looking for somewhere to stop for refreshment on a day's hike. And for those who've never spent a night in one, a day visit provides an ideal opportunity to sense what it would be like to stay there.

Austria's Alps are particularly rewarding for this. Consider the Rätikon Alps in Vorarlberg in the far west of the country. Relatively easy to get to, Brand is a small but popular resort on a bus route from the railway station at Bludenz, and from it you can either walk across meadows and through woodland to a cable car station, or take a bus to the roadhead and ride the cableway, eventually to be deposited on a dam wall overlooking the Lünersee reservoir. The large un-hut-like Douglass Hut (www.douglasshuette.at) stands next door, its restaurant brimming with visitors by day, and with walkers and trekkers when the last cable car has descended to the valley. It has excellent facilities for those who stay the night, but a day visit restricted to the restaurant won't give you much of an idea of a 'real' mountain hut. A much better plan would be to walk alongside the reservoir, then take a signed path climbing steadily to the timber-built Totalp Hut (www.totalp.at), set in a wild, almost barren landscape

Only a few metres above the Burg Hut in the Bernese Alps a memorable view rewards the walker

at 2385m (just 1¼ hours from the cable car station).

The immediate surroundings of the Totalp Hut may be as barren as suggested by its name (literally 'dead alp'), but it has exciting views onto the Lünersee 400m below and south-east along the mountain ridge that forms the border with Switzerland. Refreshments and lunchtime meals are served at tables outside, or indoors if you prefer, while above the hut rises the 2964m Schesaplana, highest of the Rätikon peaks, whose summit may be reached by a non-technical route in a little under 2 hours. With its atmospheric *Stube* and 85 places in creaky-floored dormitories, the Totalp Hut would be a great place to spend a first night in a hut, and it's so easy to get to.

Another refuge accessible by a very fine morning's walk from the Douglass Hut cable car station is the Heinrich Hueter Hut (www.hueterhuette.at), a delightful building clad with larch shingles at the foot of the Matterhorn-like Zimba. Its balcony provides a distant view of the Drei Türme of the Drusenfluh, while its location above an alp farm adds to its charm. The hut itself can sleep 110 in bedrooms and dormitories, has good showers and even an indoor climbing wall, and the bright and comfortable dining room provides a clear hint of the hut's atmosphere.

Further east, the Zillertal Alps, with Mayrhofen as the main valley base, are another great area for walking, trekking, skiing and mountaineering, with a number of huts within the reach of most active walkers. None would be better suited for a there-and-back visit than the historic Berliner Hut (www.berlinerhuette.at). Owned by the Berlin section of the German Alpine Club (Deutscher Alpenverein, DAV), it's the largest in the district, and every group I've taken there has been wowed by the hut and its outlook. Built in 1879, it is justifiably famous for the chandeliers in its panelled dining room, the lovely hallway and wide staircase more in keeping with some baronial schloss. It stands near the head of the Zemmgrund, some 3 hours' walk from Gasthof Breitlahner on the road from Mayrhofen. Not only is the hut a striking building in its own right, but its location looks out on snow-draped

> 'it is justifiably famous for the chandeliers in its panelled dining room, the lovely hallway and wide staircase more in keeping with some baronial schloss'

mountains and rushing streams, and the 8km walk to reach it from the Breitlahner bus stop is both obstacle-free and full of interest.

While still in the Zillertal Alps, there's another fine hut to visit, standing just across the Italian border at the head of the Zamsergrund – the upper reaches of the long Zillertal where buses from Mayrhofen terminate at the Schlegeis reservoir. The 2-hour walk through the Zamsergrund begins here – a delightful walk through pastures bright with alpenrose and dwarf pine, with views of waterfalls crashing down the right-hand slope. At the head of the valley, the 2246m Pfitscher Joch carries the Austrian–Italian border below the Hohe Wand

and Hochfeiler. There's an old abandoned customs house standing there, and shortly after, when you've walked between two small lakes on the Italian side, you come to the privately owned, 30-bed Pfitscherjoch-Haus, also known as Rifugio Passo di Vizze (www.pfitsch erjochhaus.com), which looks down the length of Val di Vizze.

Although Austria has numerous first-class huts and hut walks, the Italian Dolomites can challenge any alpine region for dramatic landscapes. They also have some wonderful multi-day treks, exciting via ferratas and a rich selection of *rifugi* (huts) to visit on a day's walk, a number of which are large inn-like buildings with excellent facilities. At least one boasts a sauna, but at an altitude of 2752m Rifugio Lagazuoi (www.rifugiolagazuoi.com) is more like a high-altitude hotel than a conventional mountain hut, and while it's on the route of Alta Via 1, it can also be reached by cable car from the Falzarego Pass. With stunning views of the Tofana and Cinque Torri, it has 18 beds in small rooms and 56 dorm places, and has been cared for by the same family ever since it was opened in 1965. If you've never stayed in a mountain hut before, try this one for size. But remember, not all *rifugi* will provide quite the same experience.

Without question, the best-known and most popular of Dolomite mountains is the three-turreted cluster of the Tre Cime di Lavaredo in the Dolomiti di Sesto, with Cortina the main centre and several understandably busy huts nearby, all accessible by good paths or tracks. For sheer spectacle, there's nothing quite like it. A toll road climbs up from Misurina to end in a massive car park at around 2330m by Rifugio Auronzo (www.rifugioauronzo.it), with the towering cliffs of the Tre Cime above and the Cadini pinnacles drawing attention to

Three hours' walk from the nearest road, the Berliner Hut in the Zillertal Alps boasts a chandelier-lit dining room

the south. From here, it's just a 20-minute walk to Rifugio Lavaredo (www. rifugiolavaredo.com), beyond which a bare saddle at 2457m gives an amazing view of the Tre Cime in profile.

Ahead, and some distance away, Rifugio Locatelli can be seen, with a tiny white chapel nearby. Also known as the Drei Zinnen Hut (www.dreizinnen huette.com), as a reminder that before

World War I all these mountains were Austrian, it has a direct view of the Tre Cime from its windows. Easily reached from the Auronzo car park, and with an impressive menu and generous portions served in the dining room, it is no surprise that during the summer months Locatelli makes a very popular excursion for day visitors, and is a great place to spend the night. For accommodation, it

When the crowds have departed Refuge du Lac Blanc is a magical place in which to spend the night

Blanc it must be (www.refugedulacblanc. fr). Overlooking the small mountain tarn after which it is named, and built on the slopes of the Aiguilles Rouges some 1200m above Chamonix, the refuge can be reached via several exciting trails, as well as by a combination of the Flégère cable car, Index chairlift and a well-marked high-level path. It is a privately

'a hole appeared in the clouds to reveal the huge face of the Grandes Jorasses'

owned hut with just 40 dormitory places in two buildings; it has hot showers, and a dining room that looks directly across the valley to the Chamonix Aiguilles and along the glacial highway of the Mer de Glace.

One night when I was there, a great storm erupted over the mountains. The refuge shook, lightning forked onto distant fingers of rock, and hailstones hammered on the hut roof. Then suddenly there was a lull, and a hole appeared in the clouds to reveal the huge face of the Grandes Jorasses, aloof amid the maelstrom. It was one of life's magical moments and the memory of it lives on.

has 100 dormitory places and 40 beds in smaller rooms, and a good many visitors make it their first overnight stay in an alpine hut.

Austria, Italy, Slovenia, Switzerland and France all have numerous huts worth visiting, but if you are limited to spending just a single night in one, and find yourself on a walking holiday based in or near Chamonix, then Refuge du Lac

Ten of the best-for huts

- *For a day visit: Totalp Hut (Rätikon Alps, Austria)*
- *For a first hut overnight: Refuge du Lac Blanc (Mont Blanc range, France)*
- *For an overnight on trek: Rifugio Bonatti (Tour of Mont Blanc, Italy)*
- *For climbers: Gleckstein Hut (Bernese Alps, Switzerland)*
- *For outstanding location: Cabane d'Arpittetaz (Pennine Alps, Switzerland)*
- *For views: Rifugio Locatelli (Dolomites, Italy)*
- *For sunsets: Cabane du Mont Fort (Pennine Alps, Switzerland)*
- *For starry skies: Starkenburger Hut (Stubai Alps, Austria)*
- *For solitude: Burg Hut (Bernese Alps, Switzerland)*
- *For watching wildlife: Rifugio Vittorio Sella (Gran Paradiso National Park, Italy)*

Used by trekkers on the Tour of Mont Blanc, Refuge des Mottets was converted from a dairy farm. Some of the beds are in what was once the milking parlour

Reflections in the Alpenglow

I'm never quite sure which is the most rewarding: anticipation of a day's climbing, the climbing itself, or the aftermath when you savour the memories.

Anticipation is the game that allows you to imagine perfect conditions, just the right amount of challenge, the ability to overcome all obstacles – and the view from an uncluttered summit. Reality of course rarely lives up to those expectations, while memory can be as selective as conscience allows.

But if you've had a good day out and survived to tell the tale, those moments of quiet contemplation take a lot of beating when you've dumped your rucksack, pulled off your boots, splashed your body with fresh water and slaked a well-earned thirst, knowing there's a mattress with your name on it for the night ahead. Contentment is one word for it.

So it was one glorious summer's evening at the Lindauer Hut, as the big limestone walls nearby softened in the lingering dusk. Seated on the terrace, I was served my meal to the sound of finches chittering in a grove of pine and larch trees. One flew to an upper cone, where it perched, threw back its head and called to the dying sun. I ached from days of wandering alone over meadow, ridge and summit in an orgy of pleasure, and the finch's song gave voice to the way I felt.

Meal over, shadows were swallowing screes when I went for a stroll to ease muscles still taut from a long day over rough ground. Heading across a neighbouring alp, then along a path under turrets catching the alpenglow, I turned a corner and came face to face with a tanned octogenarian in cord breeches with red braces, checked shirt and Tyrolean felt hat, who looked as though he'd emerged from a 19th-century painting by ET Compton. His pale, watery eyes shone, his leathery skin folded into innumerable creases, and a day's white stubble bristled his chin.

'Is this not the most wonderful of evenings?' he demanded, in a breathless German dialect.

I agreed that it was, and for 10 minutes or so we shared a common delight in the slumbering mountains and their gullies, the valley, the chaos of boulders at the foot of the screes, the alpenroses, streams, a small green pool, and the rim of dwarf pines that outlined a nearby moraine. He had known 60 or more Alpine summers in his 80-plus years, yet his enthusiasm was as fresh as that of a 16-year-old. It lit his features and bubbled from every pore, and I noticed, when we parted, a surprising spring to his step, as though by sharing his love of life he'd been rejuvenated.

When is a hut not a hut

With so many European languages, it's hardly surprising that there's a variety of different words to describe a mountain hut in the Alps:

cabane – French-speaking Alps (see also *refuge*)

capanna – Lepontine Alps of Switzerland (Ticino)

chamanna – Romansch-speaking Switzerland

dom – Alps of Slovenia (see also *koča*)

Hütte – Alps of Austria, Bavaria, Liechtenstein and German-speaking Switzerland

koča – Alps of Slovenia

refuge – French-speaking Alps

rifugio – Italian Alps and Lepontine Alps of Switzerland

Seen from the Stripsenjochhaus in Austria, Ellmauer Halt turns to bronze with the setting sun

2 Hut life

An overcrowded hut often means a poor night's rest...
On the other hand some huts are absolute havens of stillness and calm...

(John Barry, *Alpine Climbing*)

You don't have to be a member of an Alpine Club to stay in a mountain hut, for the vast majority are open to all-comers, whether privately owned or belonging to one of the national mountaineering organisations. Most are staffed during the main summer season, which usually extends from late June until the end of September – opening dates depend on location, altitude and, in some cases, the depth of the previous winter's snow – while some are also open for a few weeks in the late winter/ spring ski-touring season. A growing number in the most popular districts are occupied all year round. When manned, meals and drinks will be on offer; but off-season, when there's no warden in

...he beginning of the season, the Coaz Hut in the ...nina Alps may be half hidden by a wall of snow

residence, there will often be a 'winter room' available, containing little more than a few basic necessities like bunks, blankets and perhaps a wood-burning stove and a supply of fuel. At such times, the water supply may be a long way off, leading to a search for a spring or stream, or, when the ground is blanketed in snow, may involve having to melt snow or ice.

There are also those simple unguarded refuges, usually located in a remote district, where facilities are minimal and you need to carry practically everything with you, including stove, fuel and food. A friend and I once arrived at a very basic bivvy hut lodged high in the mountains, to find the door blocked by avalanche debris. It took an hour to dig a way in, only to find it contained nothing more than a few candle stubs and a box of damp matches. It was late spring, and the floor was covered in ice. A mass of snow had come down the chimney and frozen into a dome in front of the fireplace, and we found it warmer to sit outside on the roof to cook and eat. After we'd gone to bed on mattress-free boards, an avalanche targeted the hut and in the morning we had to dig our way out through the window.

Fortunately, we'd planned to be self-sufficient for a couple of weeks of climb-

Top: Where possible, huts are now providing smaller family-sized rooms
Middle: Matratzenlager (mattress rooms) like this one are common throughout the Alps
Bottom: Old-style bunk beds in the Totalp Hut in Austria's Rätikon Alps

Left: Decorative desserts are served by the warden at Berghaus Bäregg above Grindelwald, despite its remoteness
Right: In most huts there will be no choice of menu, but what you get will be both filling and tasty

ing and were able to make the most of the experience. But it is important, when planning a mountain trip – especially out of season – to do your homework first. Will the huts be open and manned? Will there be room? What facilities can be expected? Are meals provided?

Guidebooks are usually the best initial source of information on the existence and location of huts, but an increasing number of refuges now have their own websites giving up-to-date details so you can gain an idea of what to expect before finalising your plans. (See Appendix B for a list of alpine huts and their websites.) If, for example, you don't like the idea of sharing a dormitory with strangers, check out those huts that have smaller bedrooms with two, four or six bunks. Some have fresh bed linen supplied, although the cost of an overnight stay in a small room is likely to be a little higher than for dormitory accommodation, but you may feel that

a degree of privacy is worth the extra money.

Even dormitories vary, not only in size, but in the type of sleeping arrangement on offer. The traditional *Matratzenlager* – or 'mattress room' – is a large communal space with a row of anything from 8 to 30 mattresses laid side by side, while other more conventional dorms have two-tiered bunk beds. Pillows and duvets or blankets are provided, but for purposes of hygiene you must either use your own sheet sleeping bag or rent one on arrival. As there's no segregation of the sexes, a

'a certain amount of discretion is needed when sharing a dormitory full of strangers'

certain amount of discretion is needed when sharing a dormitory full of strangers, but anything more decorous than a long T-shirt as nightwear will be out of place.

If you'll be sleeping in a dormitory, the hut keeper may specify which bed space you should occupy, but if you're free to choose, try to get a place near the window and away from the door. If you have a bunk by the window you can control the air flow at night, but should you find yourself near the door, be prepared for disturbance by early risers. And keep a head torch under your pillow, for it'll be handy if you need to get up in the middle of the night for a call of nature. Most hut generators are turned off after lights-out, the bathroom may be located outside, and getting lost on the way is not to be recommended.

Bathroom facilities vary greatly. The best – and for practical reasons these will usually be found in huts located either in or within easy access of a valley – will have hot showers (mostly coin- or token-operated) and plentiful running water. Although seldom sufficient to serve the number of visitors, toilets in these 'valley huts' will be as good as those found in modest hotels, but the higher the hut, the more basic or primitive the toilets are likely to be, and more limited the opportunities for washing. There are exceptions, of course, and standards are improving year by year.

Some of the more modern huts have Wi-Fi access, but don't automatically assume that this is the case. It is also worth noting that not all huts have power sockets in which to charge mobile phones or other portable electronic devices, so you should plan your needs accordingly.

Alpenglow on Eiger, Mönch and Jungfrau seen from the Suls-Lobhorn Hut

Advance booking is essential if you wish to stay in a popular region during the high season, and it is becoming increasingly common for some huts to be fully booked several weeks or even months ahead – those in national parks and the Mont Blanc range, for example. Reservations can be made either through a central booking system such as that used by trekkers on the Tour of Mont Blanc (www.autourdumontblanc.com), or directly with individual huts by telephone. If, like me, you're no linguist, valley-based tourist offices will usually make a booking for you, but if you've left it until the last minute, some hut wardens will often phone ahead to the next refuge on your behalf. However, should you decide to make a call from your mobile phone while in the mountains, be aware that it's not always possible to get a signal.

This happened to my publisher, Jonathan Williams, and me when trekking the Tour of the Oisans one summer. Our initial plan had been to find somewhere to stay overnight in a village on the far side of a high pass, but we were checking an alternative to the standard route and misjudged the time it would take to get there. We decided to call a hut we'd be passing en route to book a couple of beds for the night. Unable to get a signal for either of our mobile phones, we arrived unannounced in the late afternoon and were met with a very frosty reception from the refuge *gardienne* (warden), who made us wait outside for half an hour like badly behaved schoolboys until she 'discovered' she had enough room and let us in. It was an unnecessary display of '*gardienne* power' as the refuge was only half full, but she made her point and we learned our lesson.

In the end it turned out to be a memorable experience, for the woman in charge soon dropped her fearsome facade, produced an excellent meal and entertained us with tales of her adventures in the Himalaya. Outside, the alpenglow was truly magical, as neighbouring

> ## 'the alpenglow was truly magical, as neighbouring mountains turned to bronze'

mountains turned to bronze and were reflected in a nearby lake. We wouldn't have had any of that if we'd made it to the village as planned.

While few huts outside the honeypot districts will be fully booked in advance, it is a matter of courtesy to call a day or two before your planned arrival as it gives the staff an idea of how many to cater for. Make sure you arrive in good time wherever possible, and it goes without saying that, if your plans change, you should phone the hut at the earliest opportunity to cancel a prior booking, otherwise walkers or climbers may be turned away unnecessarily – and the hut keeper loses income. In extreme cases, it may lead to the mountain rescue being called out to search for you.

The busiest times, of course, are in the high season and at weekends

during fine weather, when pressure on bed space is to be expected. Some wardens deal with the prospect of overcrowding by providing overflow accommodation in an annexe which may, or may not, consist of a conventional building with four walls and a roof. So I was not surprised when the guardian at the Refuge de la Leisse (www.refugedelaleisse-vanoise.com) in the Vanoise Alps told me on the phone that he was fully booked, but would find space for me and my two friends in his tented annexe. At least, that's what I thought he said – but my French is notoriously poor, so when we arrived and saw only the same three buildings that I remembered from my previous visit, and no marquee-like tent nearby, I began to wonder.

'Don't worry,' said the guardian, 'I will show you to your sleeping places in a little while.'

Half an hour later he was seen pushing a wheelbarrow up a steep slope and over a bluff, where I discovered him unloading a two-man tent and a couple of mattresses onto a patch of grass.

'Voilà!' he said. 'It's all yours. Three men, two mattresses. You will be good friends, I think.'

Advance booking should make overcrowding a rare occurrence – in theory, at least. But practice is sometimes different from theory. When an Austrian hut is completely full, the warden (*Hüttenwirt*) may allocate emergency sleeping places (*Notlager*) if, say, there's no time for a new arrival to reach alternative shelter.

In such cases, a dormitory floor, a passageway or even the space beneath a table in the dining room (*Gaststube*) may be used as a bed. If such a prospect appals you, and it's privacy you're after, you'd better turn tail and head for a valley hotel, or grab a bivvy bag and find an overhanging rock to sleep under.

House rules

Having selected a hut for the night, made your booking and arrived in good time, the first thing to do before you enter the main building is remove your outdoor boots and place them along with your trekking poles on one of the racks you'll find in the boot room or entrance porch. There will often

berge de Bionnassay on the Tour of Mont Blanc is ypical gîte d'étape with facilities similar to those und in mountain huts

No room at the inn

In the 1960s I worked for a while in the Engadine Valley, with the Bernina and Bregaglia Alps as near neighbours: snow and ice mountains in one direction, soaring rock peaks in another. Two years after I'd finished working there, I returned to introduce my 3½-month-old daughter to the Alps. Years later she remembers nothing of that visit...

Leaving my wife and daughter with friends down in the valley, I set off alone for Piz Languard, that modest 3200m walkers' mountain that rises above Pontresina with its classic view of the Bernina range, where I hoped to capture the magic of sunset and sunrise from the top.

Perched some 80m below the summit, the Georgy Hut was buzzing with voices when I arrived that September evening to be greeted by the guardian with a less-than-enthusiastic welcome. 'There is no room,' he growled. ' We are full; no beds. You should have made a reservation.'

' I don't need a bed,' I told him, 'just a drink. That's all.'

' It will be dark before you are halfway down to Pontresina.' His attitude was disdainful, and the look on his face spoke more than words. Taking the hint, I stooped to pick up my rucksack and slung it on my shoulder.

' I'm not going down tonight,' I said.' Forget the drink. I'm going up.'

He followed me to the door.' Where are you going?' he demanded.

' As I said, I'm going up. To the summit. That's where I'll spend the night.'

' Zum Gipfel? There is no shelter on the summit!' Then his voice softened. ' Look, come back. I will find a space for you somewhere.'

But I was on my way then, and called over my shoulder:' I told you - I don't need a bed. I have all I want on my back.'

All I heard then was an ill-tempered huff, the slamming of a door and the tapping of my own boots on rock.

It wasn't long before I'd pitched my tent on the very summit and sat in its entrance to capture the sun sliding into a far horizon, relishing the moment as the snowy symmetrical perfection of Piz Palü blushed and outshone her more illustrious neighbours. It was one of the best of all sunsets.

What's more, I had it all to myself.

be a supply of 'hut shoes' to change into. They could be plastic Croc-style shoes, floppy old mules or even old-fashioned clogs, all of which will be available in various sizes. If you don't fancy these, pack your own lightweight slippers to wear inside the building. But don't risk upsetting the warden by clomping through the hut in your walking boots, and if outer clothing is wet, hang waterproofs from racks in the boot room or, if there's a drying room, leave them there.

Locate the warden/hut keeper, who will probably be found in the kitchen. Check in, and show your Alpine club membership or reciprocal rights card, if you have one, to claim a discount on your overnight fee. This is valid only in huts with reciprocal arrangements. (For more information on Alpine clubs, see Chapter 5). You don't speak the language? Don't worry; before you arrange your holiday, learn a few very basic phrases and you'll be OK. Many wardens speak some English, but if they don't, you'll get by anyway. (The glossary in Appendix C lists a few key words.)

Now's the time to order any meals required, including packed lunches for the following day, and make a note of when they'll be served. The warden will probably outline any house rules, and may ask you to sign a visitors' book (the Hut Book), which keeps a log of where you came from and where you're going next day. You will be shown to your room and allocated bed space, the location of which – in climbers' huts – may depend on the time you plan to leave in the morning. In huts where rucksacks are not allowed in the dormitories, you may be given a basket in which to keep overnight essentials. As the hut's generator will be turned off after lights-out, don't forget to keep a head torch handy in case you need to get up in the night or make an early departure. To avoid disturbing others, you should pack or unpack your rucksack outside the dorm.

It's a good idea to keep a tally of food and drinks bought during your stay. In most huts, you will be asked to settle your bill the night before you leave, and as credit and debit cards are not accepted in all huts, you'd be advised to take plenty of ready cash with you.

At the majority of huts, a supply of 'hut shoes' will be found in the boot room or porch

A summary of hut conventions

- Treat huts, hut keepers and fellow hut users with respect.
- Wherever possible, reserve your accommodation in advance. Once booked, if your plans change for any reason, it is essential to phone the hut to cancel.
- On arrival, leave boots, trekking poles and wet outer clothing in the boot room or porch. Select a pair of 'hut shoes' to wear indoors.
- Locate the hut keeper to announce your arrival. Show your Alpine Club membership card or reciprocal rights card, if you have one, to claim a discount on overnight fees, and book meals and any packed lunches required for the next day. If you have dietary requirements, make these known as early as possible.
- Once your room and bed space have been allocated, make your bed using a sheet sleeping bag. Keep a head torch handy, as the hut's generator will usually be turned off after lights-out. Be considerate of others and avoid unnecessary noise in the dormitories.
- While snacks and drinks are usually available during the day, meals are served at set times, and places at table are sometimes allocated by the hut keeper.
- It is customary to pay for all services the night before leaving.
- Before departure, leave your room tidy by folding blankets or duvets, and take all litter away with you.

Sleeping and eating

At most manned huts, something resembling a restaurant-style service will be available during the day, although a set menu is the norm for breakfast and the evening meal. The majority of hut users choose half-board (bed, breakfast and evening meal), which virtually guarantees a substantial three- or four-course dinner when you really need it. Mealtimes vary from hut to hut, but dinner is usually served between 6pm and 7.30pm.

And what sort of meals might you expect? Well, perhaps not haute cuisine, except in its most literal sense, for the last thing you need after a long day in the hills is a large plate with minuscule portions of decorated artwork masquerading as a culinary treat. Mountain activities burn a lot of calories, so hut meals are usually planned with this in mind, with plenty of carbohydrate such as pasta being served. In huts owned by sections of the Austrian Alpine Club (Österreichischer

...hered round communal tables at mealtimes, hut users have a perfect opportunity to share
...eriences and route information, as at Refuge de la Flégère above Chamonix

Supplies for the Triglav Lakes Hut in Slovenia arrive on horseback

Alpenverein, ÖAV), a choice of menu is sometimes given. In addition to the items listed, a relatively low-priced *Bergsteigeressen* (literally 'mountaineer's meal') containing a minimum of 500 calories will be available to members of the ÖAV or its UK branch, the AAC. There's no choice as to what goes in it though, and the contents vary considerably, so you do tend to take pot luck and hope for the best. But it will be filling.

Outside Austria, it is rare for alpine huts to offer a choice of menu. Those who have ordered meals are usually served at large communal tables, with individual places allocated by the guardian. These mealtimes tend to be enjoyable and sometimes noisy occasions with an opportunity for visitors to get to know one another; when extra busy, two separate sittings may be needed. Jugs of drinking water are provided, and beer and wine are usually available.

The evening meal (dinner) invariably begins with a huge tureen of soup and chunks of bread, followed by the main course which is often based around spaghetti, rice, polenta (in Italy) or potatoes, with meat of one kind or another served with tinned vegetables. In Slovenia it could be a form of stew or goulash served with sauerkraut. In Switzerland you might have *rösti* (potato cakes) with a fried egg on top; or maybe *raclette* (melted cheese with potatoes boiled in their jackets). In French and Swiss huts, fresh salad or local cheeses often follow the main course, after which there'll be a simple dessert such as chocolate mousse or crème brûlée. Blueberry tart is a favourite in many districts. Given advance warning, vegetarians can be catered for, although expectations should not be raised too high as the simplest option will often be taken by the hut staff, who, as Gillian Price points out in her guidebook *Through the Italian Alps: The Grande Traversata delle Alpi*, 'have to be capable of dealing with everything from a blocked toilet, frozen pipes, refilling a diesel-powered generator, lugging firewood and provisions up steep stairs, repairing pumps and solar panels, organising rescue operations...and are expected to be gourmet chefs as well!'

A hut warden, then, is a Jack (or Jill) of all trades, with 'cook' being just one part of the job description. Love of the mountains is what entices them to spend several months of the year lodged above the clouds far from the nearest shop, and in doing so they must be prepared to meet numerous challenges undreamed of by chefs in the kitchens of valley hotels. With supplies being delivered by costly helicopter – in some cases perhaps just once or

> 'A hut warden is a Jack (or Jill) of all trades, with "cook" being just one part of the job description'

twice in a three-month season – or on the back of a mule or by a basic goods lift, where one exists, the variety and freshness of ingredients may be somewhat limited. This Jack of all trades must conjure up three-course meals for ravenous mountaineers from whatever is available, so his (or her) repertoire may not be an extensive one – although it could prove to be rather imaginative when supplies are running low. I know of several huts on popular trekking routes where the main meal served to visitors is exactly the same every night of the season. But since the majority of guests stay only one night at a time, this hardly matters, and for anyone spending a second or third consecutive night, simple alternative options are usually rustled up.

When you consider the nature of mountain activities, and the very early start required for some of them, it's not surprising that most of us are happy to get our heads down and toes up before the night is old, so guardians will often enforce a silent period (known as *Hüttenruhe* in German-speaking Alps) between 10pm and 6am to limit disturbance by the early risers – especially in high mountain huts inhabited by climbers, where the most ambitious are likely to be up and away long before 6am or,

Catching the last of the evening sunlight, walkers and climbers relax outside the Carschina Hut in the Swiss Rätikon Alps

at the very least, an hour or more before dawn.

To avoid disturbing other hut users in the early morning scrum, baskets are often provided for those essential items needed indoors, so rucksacks, ice axes, crampons, climbing ironmongery and ropes can be left in the boot room in readiness for a pre-dawn start. It's here that you need to keep your gear together so you know where to find it, for as John Barry points out, not entirely tongue-in-cheek, in his book *Alpine Climbing*, it's all too easy in the bleary-eyed post-breakfast melee for someone

to take the wrong ice axe – especially if it's better than their own – 'and it is not unknown for boots to walk away on the wrong feet.'

In climbers' huts, the serving of breakfast is often scheduled according to the needs and chosen routes of the users, so one breakfast sitting may be at 4am, while another will be served two or three hours later. On occasion, and by arrangement, the guardian will leave a Thermos of hot drink and bread wrapped in cling film for those wanting to start their route at an even more ungodly hour. Since few climbers have much of an appetite at that

The Aljažev dom in the Julian Alps of Slovenia makes a fine destination or overnight on the way to Triglav, which rises steeply above (Photo: Jonathan Willi

time of day (or night), a couple of slices of dry bread and jam, cheese or salami, washed down with a bowl of warm coffee or weak tea, will be endured rather than enjoyed. A gourmet experience before a pre-dawn start to a climb need not be anticipated. On the other hand, breakfast arrangements are much more relaxed and flexible in huts used by trekkers and walkers, with food and drink often being available from 6–8am.

Breakfasts are the standard 'continental' style, consisting of a few slices of bread and butter with jam, dried meat or cheese, and bowls of coffee, tea or hot chocolate. Cereals with milk are sometimes available, however, and in huts that are accessible from a road, it's not unusual to find fresh fruit and yogurt also on offer. Some climbers I know carry a bag of muesli pre-mixed with milk powder and, by simply adding water, manage to enhance the hut warden's breakfast offering; but if you're used to bacon and eggs before a day on the hill, you're out of luck here.

Packed lunches can usually be arranged if ordered the night before they're needed. Although comparatively expensive, in my experience the contents are often sufficient to feed two, while in all but the most remote climbers' huts, a restaurant service provides midday

'A gourmet experience before a pre-dawn start to a climb need not be anticipated'

snacks or lunches for passing walkers or early arrivals. Canned or bottled drinks are on sale in virtually every staffed hut, although prices are invariably higher than you'd pay in the valleys. In Austria and Slovenia it's not unusual for visitors to bring a supply of tea bags or coffee sachets with them, and buy a litre of hot water (*Teewasser/vroča voda*) from the warden to make their own drinks. In a number of Austrian and Swiss huts the warden will provide a supply of *Marschtee* (usually sweetened fruit tea) with which to fill your flask before leaving, at no extra cost.

There are no facilities for self-catering in most staffed huts, although there are exceptions, such as refuges managed by the French Alpine Club (Fédération Française des Clubs Alpins et de Montagne, FFCAM) which often have a room or a corner of a room set aside for visitors to prepare their own food on their own stoves as an alternative to having meals provided by the guardian. As a form of compromise, the Swiss Alpine Club (Schweizer Alpen-Club, SAC) has a rule that for a small charge, staff will cook the food a visitor has brought with them, as long as it's simple and can be quickly heated. But this facility is rarely taken, and even more rarely welcomed by the staff

A special breed

Of course, huts are not always busy, even in the height of summer among some of the most sought-after summits, for on occasion bad weather rolls in, and remains for days or even weeks at a time. Climbers desert the peaks, flee to the valleys or go in search of sunshine elsewhere. Living among rock, snow or ice way above the valley can then be a lonely existence for wardens, marooned as they are, isolated far from company. So when I appeared dripping with rain at the Rothorn Hut one day, midway through a spell of grim weather, the warden greeted my arrival with surprise. Some 1600m above Zermatt, a casual visitor that summer was a rarity.

'Where on earth have you come from?' she asked, then apologised. 'Sorry,' she said, 'but I wasn't expecting visitors. Haven't seen anyone for a week and certainly didn't imagine anyone would arrive today.' What she failed to say was, 'I didn't imagine anyone would be foolish enough to come all this way to see nothing but rain and fog,' and I didn't bother to explain that I had a book to write and could not afford to sit around in Zermatt twiddling my thumbs until the sun shone.

But imagine – living in the clouds at 3200m and seeing no one for a week! You need a focus to your days, and a lack of imagination, to put up with the isolation when storms explode all around your home.

'Any chance of a bowl of soup?' I asked. The smell coming from her kitchen was a reminder of just how long it had been since I'd eaten breakfast. In my rucksack I had a couple of cheese rolls, two bananas and some chocolate, but the prospect of soup had me salivating.

It tasted as good as it smelled; a thick lentil and vegetable soup flavoured with garlic and spices hot enough to steam my glasses. She apologised for the age of the bread, so I told her I had my own and took out the food I'd brought with me. When she saw the two bananas, her eyes popped. She hadn't seen fresh fruit all summer, so when I offered them to her I knew I'd made a friend for life.

And she was still smiling when I headed out into the murk an hour later to begin the long descent to Zermatt, although her smile only briefly lessened my sense of guilt at leaving her all alone in her fog-wrapped eyrie. But long ago I'd come to recognise that these hut wardens are a special breed, and this one certainly proved it.

themselves, as it can be extremely inconvenient during busy periods.

The hut guardian

The resident warden or guardian is the most important person at the refuge, for it is he or she who not only looks after the everyday maintenance of the hut, keeps it clean and tidy, prepares the meals, washes the dishes, serves drinks and snacks, answers queries, takes the bookings and sometimes coordinates search and rescue following an accident, but also creates the atmosphere, which is what most hut users remember.

Huts gain a reputation for being 'good' or 'bad' not necessarily because of their location, facilities or even the quality of meals provided, but by the dedication, idiosyncrasies and sociability of the person in charge. Some (the majority) make wonderful hosts, while others can be ogres. One who, to my personal knowledge, has looked after a refuge on one of the busiest routes in the Alps for at least two decades is so misanthropic that it makes me wonder if she's in the right job. Her hut is in a truly magnificent location, but I've never met anyone who has spent a night there. I never have, but hope to live long enough to experience it under the care of her eventual successor.

Having run a youth hostel long ago (in the Alps and the UK), my sympathy on the whole tends to be with the hut guardian, who needs to have 'diplomat' added to their job description – especially towards the end of a very busy season, when three

Left: A hut's reputation often rests on the personality of the warden. The gardienne at Refuge de Bellachat creates a convivial atmosphere in a stunning location
Right: Some hut wardens are professional mountain guides. Elia Negrini at Rifugio Longoni is one. Here he offers welcome advice to one of his guests

or four months of long days and very short nights tend to leave nerves a little ragged. So my plea is for all visitors to have patience and good humour and to treat the guardian with the respect they'd hope to be shown in return. Common courtesy goes a long way.

I took a group to one of my favourite alpine huts for lunch one day. The first two members of the group to arrive before me were unable to get served when they asked the guardian for a drink. When I arrived a few minutes later I was served immediately. It had nothing to do with the fact that I was the leader. I simply greeted the man behind the counter with 'Bonjour!' That's all it took.

By far the majority of hut wardens are unfailingly cheerful, hard-working enthusiasts – perhaps a little eccentric (as you'd need to be to choose such a challenging lifestyle in an equally challenging environment) but ever welcoming to their guests. Some are student volunteers, or wannabe guides. Some of the best are enterprising career wardens who, with their partner and/or family, look after the same hut every summer, year in and year out, and have a different job when the season ends. The large Jamtal Hut (www. jamtalhuette.at) in Austria's Silvretta Alps is a good example of this continuity of care, for it has been looked after by three

> 'hut wardens are unfailingly cheerful, hard-working enthusiasts'

generations of the Lorenz family since it was first opened in 1882. A good many hut keepers work as ski instructors in the winter; one I know is an accountant for six months of the year – how's that for variety? Another goes trekking in the Himalaya. But as a new season approaches, whatever they've been doing during the closed period, they'll be shovelling snow from the door, thawing frozen pipes and stocking up with supplies for the next few months to make sure all is well when the first visitors arrive.

My wife Min and I were in Austria one summer long ago making a hut-to-hut crossing of the Ötztal Alps. Late one afternoon we arrived at the sturdy, stone-built Braunschweiger Hut (www.braunschweiger-huette.at), set upon rocks at 2759m with a splendid view across the Mittelbergferner glacier to the district's highest peak, the Wildspitze. When we pushed open the door of the boot room, we were greeted by a Sherpa from Nepal who was working there for the summer as assistant to the warden. He served our meal that evening, and when his duties were over, sat talking with us until lights-out, sharing a common love of mountains, not only those here in the Alps but also those in his home country, as a result of which we've since made numerous treks together in the Himalaya.

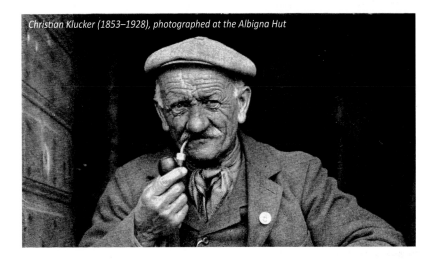

Christian Klucker (1853–1928), photographed at the Albigna Hut

CHRISTIAN KLUCKER,
MOUNTAIN GUIDE AND HUT KEEPER

Over the years, many mountain guides have been responsible for the planning, siting and even maintenance of alpine huts, and a number of guides and former guides have taken on the role of hut keeper. One of the best known was the Engadine-based Christian Klucker.

Born in 1853 in Val Fex, a minor tributary of the Engadine, Klucker was not only a popular guide during the 'silver age' of mountaineering, pioneering numerous new routes in the Bregaglia Alps and elsewhere, but when the Bernina section of the SAC was founded in 1891, he also became entrusted with the supervision of its huts, for which he was well qualified. He had supervised the building of the Forno Hut on behalf of his friend and benefactor Theodor Curtius in 1889, and later became its guardian. At one time, no fewer than five huts were in his care: the Rascher, Jürg Jenatsch, Boval, Tschierva and Mortèl (which was later replaced by the Coaz).

But Klucker had very fixed ideas, and during his time at the Forno Hut he would allow no playing cards to be used there; and if any were found, he'd toss them on the fire. 'Only weak creatures resort to "Jass" in the high Alps, when they have such ample opportunity for devoting themselves to it down in the valley,' he scoffed.

The hills are alive...

Edging along a narrow terrace that ran across the face of the mountain, we caught sight of a hut about 1km away and 200m below. A blob of roofed stone, it was dwarfed by slabs and boulders that lay among tarns in the midst of a granite wilderness. From a distance it appeared to be deserted, and when we eventually arrived at the door our suspicions proved correct; the hut was deserted – apart, that is, from the guardian who emerged from the shadows rubbing his eyes with no attempt to hide the fact that he'd just fallen out of bed. It was mid afternoon, and my long-time climbing partner Alan and I had been on the go for 6 hours.

'Bonjour,' yawned the guardian. 'You look hot.'

It was hot, and heat from the early September sun bounced off the smooth granite to emphasise the fact.

'Any chance of a beer?'

'It's in the fridge,' said the guardian, and he led us round the back of the hut where several bottles were submerged in a spring-fed pool. He handed one to Alan, another to me, and took one for himself, then pulled a pen-knife from his pocket and yanked the top from each one.

Never did beer taste so good.

Rucksacks slid from our backs to lean against the wall, and with sweat-stained shirts draped over rocks we lowered ourselves to the ground to relax against the front of the building – with a second bottle waiting to be drained, clutched in our hands or held against a burning brow. I'd drink that one slowly, to allow the flavour to settle.

After a few short, monosyllabic questions about where we'd come from and whether we planned to stay the night, the guardian fell silent and let the afternoon's peace settle around us.

Trapped in a landscape of stone and still water, there were practically no sounds. No birds sang. No streams gurgled. No stones clattered into a far-off gully. If it had not been for the blood coursing through my veins, the only certainty that I'd not grown deaf was the distant thrum that spoke of the Earth spinning in space.

After some time, a shadow moved across my face. Opening one eye, I saw the guardian slip quietly into the hut and was vaguely aware of his bare feet padding on the stone floor. Moments later he reappeared, carrying a flute in his right hand, its silver dazzling in the sunshine. Choosing a rocky perch above the nearest small lake, 20 paces from Alan and me, he settled, cross-legged, like a bearded maestro facing an audience full of expectation. I nudged Alan, and when he opened his eyes I nodded towards the flautist, who now had our undivided attention.

This would be good! Imagine – big bold mountains reflecting the sun; an azure lake, a mind at peace fully receptive to the subtleties of some lyri-cal composition. The acoustics would be interesting here at 2300m, with the music echoing across the lake to produce a delayed stereo effect. It would be a unique experience, one to savour. A solitary flute to ser-enade and soften a harsh wilderness. Mozart, perhaps? Or something modern?

I took another sip of beer, leaned back against the hut's wall and closed my eyes again, then held my breath as I pictured the guardian raising the instrument to his face, one elbow at right angles to his body. He'd mois-ten his lips with his tongue, then launch into his repertoire.

But the peace of the mountains was rudely shattered – and with it our anticipation – as the guardian, a musical novice, practised his scales. Over and over and over again.

The flute screeched, and badly constructed notes spattered on warm granite slabs and scratched at our ears. It was an insult both to music and to the natural harmonies of the landscape. So we drained our beer and scampered to some far corner of the mountains where the scrooping could not be heard. And silence returned.

We understood, then, why the hut was empty.

Paying for the privilege

The fee for staying in a hut owned by one of the national Alpine Clubs is divid-ed between the price of a bed and the cost of meals and drinks. Income from bed fees usually goes to the club which owns the hut, while that from the sale of meals and drinks forms an important part of the warden's income – the war-den usually being self-employed. While providing value for money, the expense of transporting food and equipment to remote huts explains why costs are perhaps higher than you might expect to pay in similar valley-based accommodation. However, members of Alpine Clubs and other organisations affiliated to the International Union of Alpine Associations (UIAA) receive a reduction on overnight fees – which varies from country to country. So if you plan to spend most of your climbing or trekking holiday overnighting in huts, membership of an Alpine Club could be of financial benefit. But note that in huts belonging to the Italian Alpine Club (Club Alpino Italiano, CAI), members should be of the same nationality as the club they belong to in order to claim discounts.

Membership of the UK branch of the Austrian Alpine Club (www.aacuk. org.uk) is the cheapest option for UK-based climbers and walkers, for members not only receive a reduction in the price of overnight accommodation but are automatically insured for emergency mountain rescue, medical treatment and

worldwide repatriation. Alternatively, you can enjoy reduced overnight rates with a reciprocal rights card, which can be bought (by members only) from the British Mountaineering Council (BMC, www.thebmc.co.uk), although you'd need several hut-nights to cover the cost of both BMC membership and a discount card.

Or you could save money by taking a tent, doubling the weight of your rucksack and heading in search of a pitch with a view. But don't try sneaking into a hut to use its facilities when the guardian's back is turned.

Not huts – *Berghotels* and *gîtes d'étape*

As well as the many hundreds of mountain huts spread across the alpine chain, simple dormitory accommodation can also be found in cable car stations, in the attics of hotels and even in restaurants. All of these will have much better

---

The Hut Book

Most huts belonging to the various Alpine Clubs have a 'Hut Book' – a large visitors' book in which all who stay should provide their name and home address, and leave a record of where they've come from and where they intend to go. This is a safety precaution that could be of help in the event of an accident or of someone going missing. In climbers' huts, route details and conditions on the mountain or crag are sometimes added, while in huts mostly used by walkers and trekkers, lengthy comments and amusing cartoons describing people or incidents on the trail can sometimes add to the interest of fellow hut users.

...es are simple valley-based walkers' hostels offering hut-like facilities. Le Moulin, at Les Tsserands in the Chamonix valley, is used by trekkers on the Tour of Mont Blanc

amenities than would have been acceptable 60 years or so ago, when Douglas Milner, a stalwart of the Alpine Club, was happy to recommend the old stables near the Hotel du Montenvers overlooking the Mer de Glace, which had been converted into dormitories where a night on a mattress could be had cheaply. But he added, 'you should take your own DDT.' (*Mont Blanc and the Aiguilles*)

Standards of accommodation move on, and nowadays literally scores of privately owned *gîtes d'étape* and a number of rustic mountain inns (*Berghotels* or *Berghäuser*) – some of which may be as old as, or even older than, the very first huts – make suitable low-level lodgings for anyone active in the Alps, without the need for DDT.

Found throughout France and French-speaking cantons of Switzerland, a gîte d'étape is best described as a walker's

> 'a gîte d'étape is best described as a walker's hostel'

hostel, or simple *pension*, usually located in valleys and villages. As with mountain huts, they are great places in which to meet like-minded outdoor folk, for guests take meals together, which helps create a happy atmosphere. A *gîte* performs a similar function to a hut (in fact it's often difficult to distinguish between the two), with beds in communal dormitories and meals prepared and served by the owner. Unlike a number of huts, however, indoor toilets and hot showers are provided as standard, and many also have facilities for self-catering. The long distance Grande Randonnée (GR) trails of France are peppered with these *gîtes*, as are sections of the Walker's Haute Route between Chamonix and Zermatt, and several of them are patronised by trekkers on the Tour of Mont Blanc.

The mountain inns of Austria, Switzerland and South Tyrol are rather different from *gîtes d'étape* in architectural style, location and ambience, and have an attraction all their own. No more sophisticated than old hotels, 'In America, they would have been shut down or rebuilt 40 years ago' – so said writer Marcia R Lieberman as long ago as the 1980s (*Walking in Switzerland the Swiss Way*). Fortunately, 'old Europe' is not so anxious to dispense with tradition, and a rich heritage of these rustically romantic buildings with their gingham curtains, pine-panelled walls and carved furniture adds something special to journeys across parts of the Alps. In some respects they have an affinity with a few of the older Austrian huts, for in addition to twin-bedded rooms, most will have dormitory accommodation available, even if it's located in an annexe or outhouse.

In the Swiss Alps, a number of these *Berghotels* can be found above Zermatt, and also in the neighbouring Saastal, where the charming Berghotel

About 14km from Klosters, Berghaus Vereina is one of the more modern Berghotels, built in 1930

Almagelleralp (www.almagelleralp.ch) is reached by a walk of about 1½ hours from Saas Almagell. With a few double rooms and three small dormitories, views are extraordinary in every direction, and the place seems to inhabit a world of its own.

The Bernese Alps also have their fair share of *Berghotels*: in the Lötschental, in the wild Gasterntal near Kandersteg, in the little hanging valley of the Blumental above Mürren, at Alpiglen below the Eiger, and at the head of the Lauterbrunnen Valley, for example, there stand a number of handsome dark-timbered buildings, each of which offers a memorable overnight experience far from the nearest road, their uneven floors, ill-fitting doors and big open fires making a stark contrast to the more ritzy hotels that line the streets of many an alpine resort. Some do not even have electricity, so dinner is served by candlelight, and en suite facilities consist of little more than a Victorian pitcher and a glazed porcelain basin, with a communal toilet located along a corridor.

A particular favourite is Berghaus Vereina (www.berghausvereina.ch) in the Silvretta Alps. As remote as a good many mountain huts, it stands on a 1943m knoll at the junction of the Vereina and Vernela valleys, some 14km from Klosters. Built only in 1930, it's more modern than some, but it retains the atmosphere of a previous generation of *Berghotels*, replacing an old wooden SAC hut run by the grandparents of the present owner, and offers a choice of bedrooms and dormitory places. Its location is perfect as a base from which to explore some very fine valleys, to climb a number of fairly straightforward peaks, and cross passes that lead deep into the heart of the region, where more conventional alpine huts can be found that serve trekkers and climbers.

On one of my visits, a figure suddenly appeared outside with a huge alpine horn, which he placed on a nearby bluff and bounced echoes of his limited repertoire of notes across the valley. I've no idea where he came from, for I'm sure he was not staying at the *Berghaus*, and when darkness fell he simply disappeared.

On another occasion, when trekking the Alpine Pass Route, I found my way to a classic old *Berghaus* below the Blümlisalp, where a choir of yodellers happened to be spending several nights. At mealtimes, between each course, they would rattle the windows with Swiss folk songs – a dozen lubricated yodellers building their appetites and deadening any thought of conversation. It was free entertainment – if you like that sort of thing. But it was all part of a traditional Swiss mountain experience. And an experience is what many of us seek when we head for the hills.

Unexpected ad hoc 'entertainment' at Berghaus Vereina

3 Top ten huts

Evenings spent in a mountain hut are the most sublime and intense that life holds

(Primo Levi, *Bear Meat*)

A ll who stay in mountain huts will have their own favourites, based, no doubt, on personal experience. The following list (in alphabetical order, rather than a scale from one to ten) represents a tiny fraction of those in which I've spent a night or two during walks, treks or climbs in just about every alpine district over many years. Most of those that made the shortlist happen to be traditional, old-fashioned refuges, often with limited or very modest facilities – which, perhaps, reflects an old-fashioned 'romantic' approach to mountains that may not be shared by readers of this book. But I make no apologies for that! As for the guidebooks listed, these are the titles that have a specific use relevant to the huts described; there may be others available.

Cabane d'Arpitettaz (2786m)

Hut essentials

Location
Pennine Alps, Switzerland

Valley base
Zinal

Hut capacity
32 places

Staffed
from June to late September.

Tel
+41 (0)27 475 40 28

Website
www.arpitettaz.ch

Guidebooks
Walking in the Valais **(Cicerone Press),**
Valais Alps East **(Alpine Club)**

In July 1864, Edward Whymper, AW Moore and their guides Christian Almer and Michel Croz left Zinal to make their way into the Arpitetta cirque in search of a herdsman's chalet, where they planned to spend the night before attempting to cross the Moming Pass. 'The Moming glacier opened out broadly and grandly in front of us as we advanced,' wrote Moore in *The Alps in 1864*, 'backed by the wonderful cliffs of the Weisshorn, Schalihorn, Rothorn, and Lo Besso. The tops of the peaks were in the clouds, but we saw enough to lead us to believe that the scene presented by the amphitheatre... has few equals in the Alps.' Anyone who

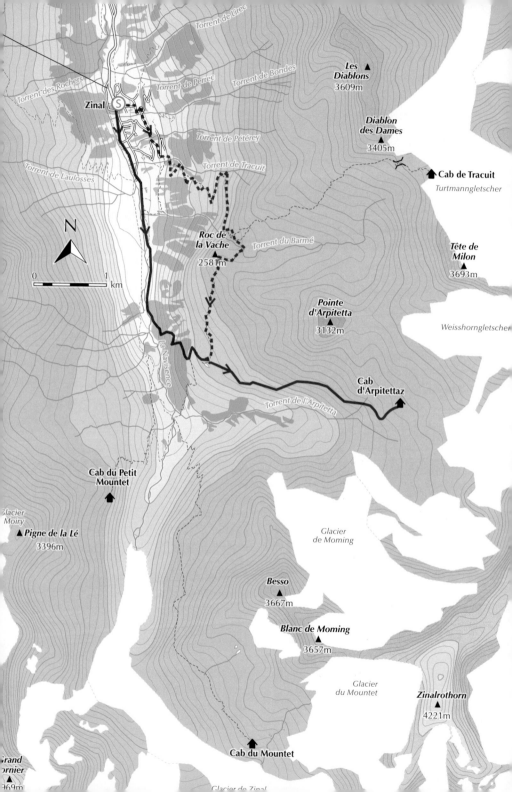

Les
Diablons
3609m

Diablon
des Dames
3405m

Cab de Tracuit
Turtmanngletscher

Tête de
Milon
3693m

Torrent de Lires

Torrent de Perrec

Torrent de Bondes

Torrent des Rochers

Zinal

Torrent de Pétérey

Torrent de Tracuit

Torrent de Laulosses

N

0   1
         km

Roc de
la Vache
2581m

Torrent du Barmé

Pointe
d'Arpitetta
3132m

Weisshorngletscher

Torrent de l'Arpitetta

Cab
d'Arpitettaz

la Navisence

Cab du Petit
Mountet

Glacier
Moiry

Pigne de la Lé
3396m

Glacier
de Moming

Besso
3667m

Blanc de Moming
3657m

Glacier
du Mountet

Zinalrothorn
4221m

Grand
ornier

Cab du Mountet

Glacier de Zinal

369m

A group of walkers leave the Arpitettaz Hut on a day of snowy brilliance. Zinal is about 3 hours away.

has visited the Cabane d'Arpitettaz would readily agree with him, for the great wall of rock, snow and ice, rising to a lofty pelmet of corniced ridge, has created a scene of spectacular beauty. It really is one of the finest of all alpine views, and as a backdrop to a mountain hut it could not be improved.

In 1953, almost 100 years after Whymper and Moore were here, the Arpitetta (or Arpitettaz) Hut was built by seven Val d'Anniviers guides with a view to encouraging mountaineering in what is without question one of the most beautiful but more remote corners of the Pennine Alps. A small refuge constructed of

stone with a traditional design, it was enlarged and upgraded in 2016. Owned by the Swiss Alpine Club (Schweizer Alpen-Club, SAC) and staffed by volunteers, the hut provides soup, drinks and occasional snacks for visitors, but no meals. It has a kitchen for self-catering, and is also open but unguarded throughout the winter.

I took a group there once after a dump of late summer snow, and the light reflected off the surrounding mountains seemed to fill the building with an intense glow. The part-time warden plied us with mugs of the finest hot chocolate in all Switzerland, while we gazed out of the window at a view it was impossible to ignore. Life, I figured, was at this moment as good as it gets, and I could have stayed there for ever. Maybe I should have done, for several hours later my group and I stumbled into our Zinal hotel to find the staff gathered in front of a television set as the drama of 9/11 was played out for all the world to see. We'd gone from one reality to the horror of another, and life would never be quite the same again.

Approach routes

❶ The small mountaineering centre of **Zinal** lies near the roadhead at the southern end of Val d'Anniviers, a valley hailed as the grandest or greatest of the Pennine Alps. This is where the two main approach routes begin, both of which will take 4–4½ hours. The most direct of these strikes upvalley to the end of the road, from where a track cuts through the meadows of Pla de la Lé. Continuing below a waterfall coming from Alp La Lé, the way then forks left,

crosses a footbridge and climbs among lush vegetation to reach a charming little lake near the buildings of the Arpitetta alp (2½ hours). The head of Val d'Anniviers looks magnificent from here, with Dent Blanche and the Grand Cornier dominating.

A trail now climbs into the Arpitetta cirque along the left-hand slope, with views growing more impressive with every step: Weisshorn ahead, Schalihorn, Zinalrothorn and rocky tower of Lo Besso, and an arc of glaciers spreading to the right. Several streams are crossed before a final steep haul up a prow of rock and grass brings you to the door of **Cabane d'Arpitettaz**.

❷ The alternative approach goes via the acclaimed viewpoint of the 2581m **Roc de la Vache**. There's a steep ascent to the Roc and an equally steep descent from it, before the way eases into the mouth of the Arpitetta cirque to join the more direct route near the Arpitetta alp.

Cabane d'Arpitettaz, not far from the 'hovel' in which Whymper spent a night in 1864

Ascents

With the Weisshorn looming above and behind the hut, the west face of this prominent 4000er is an obvious attraction. There are several fine routes on this, including the classic Younggrat, named after Geoffrey Winthrop Young, who pioneered the route in 1900.

Neighbouring huts

❶ Reached by a steep walk through the Combautanna cirque (visited on the way to the Roc de la Vache), the large Cabane de Tracuit is located on the ridge near the Tracuit col at 3256m, between the Diablon des Dames and Tête de Milon, about 4–4½ hours from Zinal.

❷ Another approach route of 4–4½ hours goes along the east flank of the Zinal valley (the upper reaches of Val d'Anniviers) to gain the popular Cabane du Mountet (2886m), situated near the junction of the Mountet and Zinal glaciers with a direct view of the Obergabelhorn. It's a demanding walk on a well-engineered path, but safeguarded in places with fixed chains.

❸ The shortest and easiest of hut walks leading out of Zinal takes you to the privately owned Cabane du Petit Mountet in a little under 2 hours. It stands at 2142m on the west bank moraine of the shrinking Zinal glacier, with an impressive number of high mountains on show.

The Roc de la Vache route to Arpitettaz passes this ruined hut

Hut essentials

Location
Massif des Écrins, Dauphiné Alps, France

Valley base
Vallouise

Hut capacity
22 places

Staffed
from mid June to mid September

Tel
+33 (0)4 92 23 39 48

Website
www.refugedesbans.ffcam.fr

Guidebooks
Écrins National Park, Tour of the Oisans: GR54 and *100 Hut Walks in the Alps* (Cicerone Press); *Écrins Park* (West Col)

After the Mont Blanc range, the Écrins massif is the highest in France, a magnificently wild region in which more than 100 peaks rise to well over 3000m, their deep valleys sliced by frantic torrents. Although a number of its mountains are hung about with glaciers, many of their walls are too steep to contain either permanent snow or ice. These are connoisseurs' mountains, their routes cherished by a select band of climbers who prefer their comparative sense of isolation to the honeypot districts further north. Even so, places like La Bérarde and Ailefroide are real climbers' hotspots, while walkers have a somewhat broader catchment area to explore. For walkers and experienced trekkers there's much to discover in the valleys of the

Écrins National Park, with the multi-day Tour of the Oisans (GR54) being a major challenge. Among several huts visited by GR54, Refuge des Bans is an optional extra, but for those of us who appreciate traditional refuges with a convivial atmosphere, the diversion is well worth taking.

Located at the head of the Vallée de l'Onde (also known as the Vallée d'Entraigue), Refuge des Bans belongs to the Briançon section of the French Alpine Club (Fédération Française des Clubs Alpins et de Montagne, FFCAM). A small, unashamedly old-fashioned hut built of stone, it has barely changed since it was first opened for business in 1946. It has a single dormitory with 22 places, a solar-heated shower, a communal dining room and a small terrace with a direct outlook downvalley. But above the hut, a rugged arc of mountains is crowned by the great grey bulk of Les Bans, while across the valley to the south, Pic de Bonvoisin captures the attention with its small hanging glaciers. All in all, it's a savage scene to look out upon: a wilderness of rock and

'it's a savage scene to look out upon'

crashing streams, softened only by a few hardy plants, and the hut is perfectly situated to make the most of it.

The first time I called there I was researching routes for a guide to the

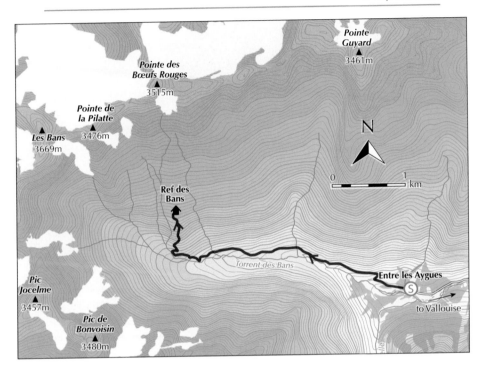

Écrins National Park. Min and I traipsed up the valley in gusting wind and intermittent rain. Low clouds blocked the light and shut off any prospect of views, and when we finally arrived and pushed open the door, we discovered that the guardian had left for the season. As we'd not brought any provisions with us, we turned tail and headed back downvalley in a sullen mood.

But next time – ah, that was different! Two of us were making a Tour of the Oisans, sunlight was trapped in the valley and every stream and waterfall glistened. We reached the hut in good time, and having checked in we sat on the stone wall outside, legs dangling over the valley, cold drinks in hand, content in the knowledge that we had nowhere else to go that day. The hut was half full, and when evening drew in, a homely atmosphere was created under flickering lights as the sounds and smells of cooking drifted from the kitchen. The guardian was eager to share his knowledge of the area in response to every enquiry, but warned that the weather was due to change next day. That night I lay in my sleeping bag, warm, comfortable and cosy, as a storm shook the building and rain thundered on the dormitory roof. Outside, it was as if the mountains were

An unashamedly traditional hut, Refuge des Bans has changed little since it was opened in 1946

falling apart, and not for the first time that summer I was thankful not to be curled up in a bivvy bag under a rock.

Approach route

A straightforward approach makes this a favourite outing for visitors staying in Vallouise, from where a narrow road ending in a parking area at **Entre les Aygues** saves what otherwise would be an additional 2½ hours of walking, much of it on tarmac. Those without a car might consider taking a taxi, in order to spend extra time at the hut.

From the roadhead car park, a sign directs the way through stands of birch and larch on the right-hand side of a gravelly plain. Beyond this, the path rises through an increasingly wild valley in long switchbacks, and roughly halfway to the hut it crosses a small pasture running with streams. As you progress deeper

into the valley, **Refuge des Bans** may be seen perched on a rocky knoll ahead. The trail twists up towards it, a fixed cable safeguarding one exposed section, before making the final approach in company with a lively torrent that cascades through a channel of rock. Allow 1½–2 hours from Entre les Aygues.

Ascents

Being the highest hereabouts at 3669m, Les Bans is an obvious attraction for climbers, its great slabs providing a choice of routes (see the topos in the hut). Pic de Bonvoisin (3480m), the 3457m Pic Jocelme and Pointe des Bœufs Rouges (3515m) are also worthy of attention. There are no other refuges easily accessible from here, and walking is pretty much limited to a there-and-back route from the roadhead.

The final approach to Refuge des Bans
accompanies this riotous mountain torrent

Refuge de Bellachat
(2152m)

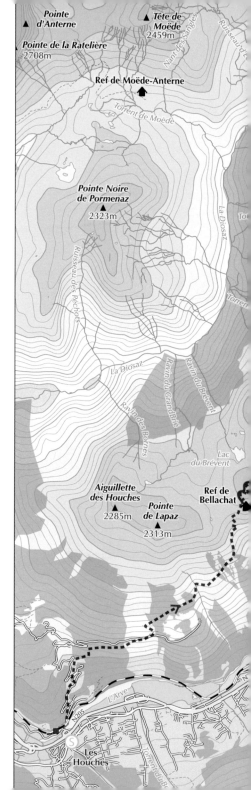

Hut essentials

Location
Mont Blanc range, France

Valley base
Chamonix

Hut capacity
28 places

Staffed
from late June to late September

Tel
+33 (0)4 50 53 46 99

Website
www.refugebellachat.com

Guidebooks
Tour of Mont Blanc and *100 Hut Walks in the Alps* (Cicerone Press)

Overlooked as an overnight option by the vast majority of trekkers tackling the Tour of Mont Blanc (TMB), who, at best, linger there for refreshment before making their final descent of the trek, Refuge de Bellachat is one of my all-time favourite huts. A small, privately owned, timber-clad refuge tucked on a narrow shelf some 370m below the summit of Le Brévent, its 28 mattresses are crammed into three small dormitories, there's only one outdoor toilet, and cold water for washing comes from two taps over a ceramic sink in an outhouse. But these limitations are more than compensated for by the warm welcome offered by the *gardienne* (warden), whose father built the hut and opened

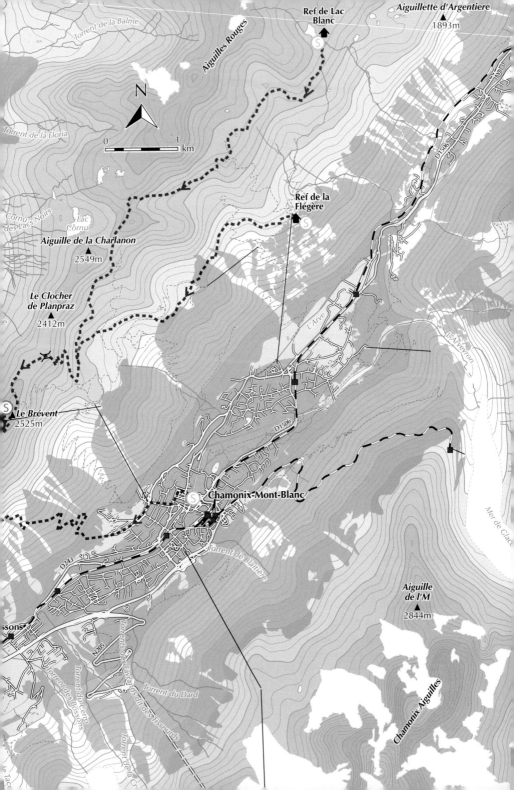

'A full moon rose above Mont Blanc and hung there to spread its light on rock and ice alike'

it for business in 1983. In addition to the friendly welcome, excellent refreshments are served to passing walkers at the terrace tables, while appetising meals can be expected by those staying overnight. Then there's the sensational view of Mont Blanc and the Aiguilles, with the trunk-like Bossons glacier seen just across the valley, adding to the appeal, while Chamonix itself lies 1100m vertically below the hut terrace, giving the place an airy bird's-eye view.

In the first edition of his Cicerone guide to the TMB, published in 1977, the late Andrew Harper spoke of Bellachat as 'the site of a derelict building, once offering well-earned refreshment to the walkers coming up the steep path from Chamonix.' The 'derelict building' was, in fact, an earlier refuge that had replaced an even older one, used by muleteers and their clients on their way from Chamonix to Le Brévent, which was destroyed by a storm in 1926. In the late 1970s, Georges Balmat began to build on the same site; and by the time a reprint of the fourth edition of Harper's *Tour of Mont Blanc* was published shortly before

he died in 2001, Harper was describing the refuge that rose from the ruins as being 'not only delightfully situated but [having] a warm friendliness [which] exudes from the place.' Nowadays, a night spent at Refuge de Bellachat ensures the TMB ends on a high note, but it will need booking in advance.

Having an excuse to keep re-walking the TMB in order to update and refresh the guidebook, a night at the Bellachat refuge is one I always relish, whether descending to it on the 'standard' anti-clockwise tour, or climbing up to it from Les Houches when tackling the route in the opposite direction. The warm smile of welcome, the certainty of a simple but filling meal, the familiar dorm, and an unbeatable terrace that rewards with a view worth a king's ransom – all these things put it high on my top ten list. I was there recently with my wife and daughter, for both of whom it was their first visit, and as expected they were as captivated by it as I am. A full moon rose above Mont Blanc and hung there to spread its light on rock and ice alike. In our dorm, fellow trekkers remained snug in their blankets while I crept out onto the terrace to experience once more the magic of our lodging perched high upon a moonlit mountain.

Approach routes

❶ The shortest and most direct approach comes from the 2525m summit of **Le Brévent**, one of the classic vantage points from which to study Mont Blanc. It can be reached by two-stage cable car from Chamonix, followed by a steep descent to **Refuge de Bellachat** in a little over an hour.

② Walkers on the Tour of Mont Blanc usually make their way to Refuge de Bellachat by following the Grand Balcon Sud from either **Refuge de la Flégère** or **Refuge du Lac Blanc**. The two routes join above Planpraz, and climb easily at first, then more steeply to the rocky Col du Brévent where the route of la Grande Traversée des Alpes (better known as GR5) is met. A rocky hollow leads to a pair of metal ladders, bringing you up to a piste that rises to a junction just below the summit of **Le Brévent**. Here, a signed path plunges down to Les Houches, with

Perched on a narrow shelf 1100m above Chamonix, Refuge de Bellachat may have limited facilities, but the ambience and location more than compensate

a short spur cutting left to **Refuge de Bellachat** – about 4½ hours from La Flégère. ❸ Any approach from the Chamonix valley will inevitably involve a steep ascent. TMB walkers tackling the route 'against the grain' on a clockwise circuit will need something like 3½ hours for the 1100m climb from **Les Houches**. However, coming from **Chamonix** and **Les Bossons** there's another route of 3–3½ hours which breaks off from the Petit Balcon Sud and climbs above Plan Lachat at 1574m in a series of tight zigzags to gain **Refuge de Bellachat** from the south-east.

Onward routes

Above the refuge, there's a path heading north-west to the Aiguillet des Houches, and another option from the trail that climbs to Le Brévent, providing an opportunity to break away to visit the lovely Lac du Brévent.

But an interesting hut-to-hut route, taking about 4½–5 hours, follows GR5 to Col du Brévent and continues heading north, before descending to the ruined Chalets d'Arlevé on the way to the Moëde valley. Here, the privately owned Refuge de Moëde-Anterne sits among pastures at the foot of the impressive Rochers des Fiz.

The view from the terrace at Refuge de Bellachat includes Mont Blanc and most of the Chamonix Aiguilles

Rifugio Bolzano/Schlernhaus (2437m)

Hut essentials

Location
Dolomites, Italy

Valley base
Siusi

Hut capacity
120 places

Staffed
from June to early October

Tel
+39 0471 612024

Website
www.schlernhaus.it

Guidebooks
Walking in the Dolomites and *Shorter Walks in the Dolomites* (Cicerone Press)

A group of elegant stone buildings make up the marvellous Rifugio Bolzano, otherwise known as the Schlernhaus ('the house on the Schlern mountains'). It stands upon the vast high-altitude pastures of the *altopiano* plateau, also known as the Sciliar, which was once a coral reef – around 230 million years ago, that is, well before the Alps were formed. Nowadays, cows and horses graze there in summer, seemingly oblivious to both the geological history and the spectacular Dolomite views, says Gillian Price.

In summer it's a popular destination, despite the demanding 1000m height gain required to reach it. But savvy visitors go to stay the night and enjoy the stunning

With its spectacular view of the neighbouring Catinaccio, Rifugio Bolzano is also known as the Schlernhaus (Photo: Gillian Price)

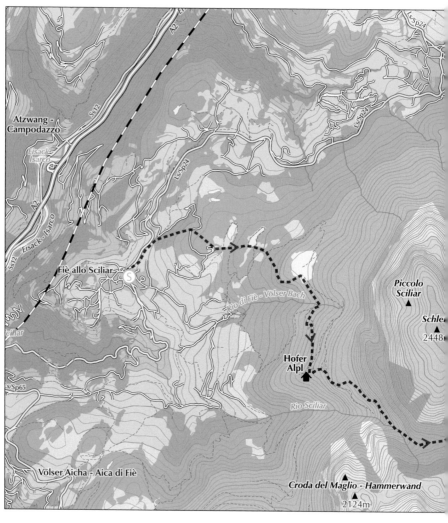

evening colours on the neighbouring Catinaccio, studded with rock turrets that glow at sunset with gorgeous pinks and reds – the *enrosadira*. This effect comes courtesy of the legendary King Laurin, whose well-tended rose garden once covered the rocky slopes. Laurin had kidnapped a princess, but when she was later rescued he fell into despair at the loss of his beloved, cursing his rose bushes and accusing them of leading the rescuers into his kingdom. He turned the roses to stone,

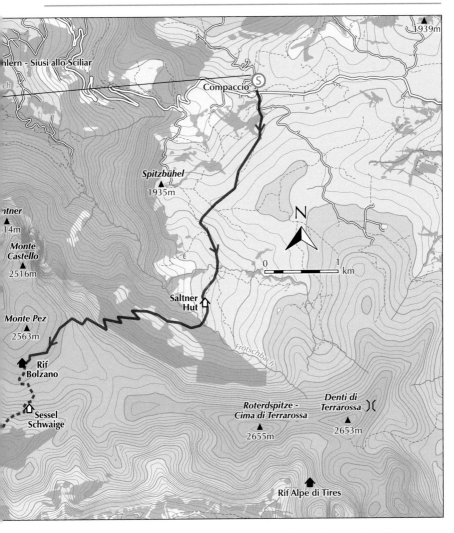

never again to bloom by day or night. However, he overlooked the in-between times, so the roses still 'bloom' ever so briefly at sunrise and sunset.

Rifugio Bolzano is a comfortable hut run by a local family with an army of help-ers, and supplies are brought up on a mechanised goods lift. There are beds in cosy rooms as well as 100 places in light-filled dormitories in the annexe, although hot showers are not on the list of facilities. The original building dates back to 1885,

Torre Venezia dominates the route to Rifugio Vazzoler AV1 Stage 7 (Photo: Gillian Price)

and was the work of local mountaineering pioneer Johann Santner, the first to make the ascent (in 1880) of what is now known as Punta Santner, the Sciliar's trademark 2414m tooth-like point. The old hut could host as many as 50 guests, which would have included paying mountaineers, guides and porters, while horses (for the ladies) were put up in the annexe.

Approach routes

❶ The most popular, and the shortest, access route strikes out from **Compaccio**, a cable car ride from Siusi, where a series of well-signed lanes and paths lead south-west up across the undulating Alpe di Siusi, touching on the summer eatery of the **Saltner Hut**. A refreshment stop is in order here, as next comes a steep slog on the zigzagging Touristenweg to reach **Rifugio Bolzano**. About 3 hours should suffice.

❷ The most memorable way to approach the hut is rather longer – 4–5 hours, and a height gain of 1580m – although it could be broken with an overnight stay at the family-run Hofer Alpl, a typical Tyrolean building approximately halfway. The route begins at **Fiè allo Sciliar**, the castle village nestling below the Sciliar's western flanks. Clear lanes and paths head due east to climb gently past lakes and through forest to the landmark Peter Frag crucifix, and the opening to a corridor gully. This marks the start of a curious ancient livestock route, where planks laid over a stream and a rocky floor facilitate the passage of cows and horses to summer pasture. After a welcome refresh-ment stop at the cheery **Sessel Schwaige**, a final effort concludes on the verge of the plateau near **Rifugio Bolzano**.

Ascents

The classic peak here, and the one whose ascent is, quite frankly, almost compulsory, is Monte Pez. At 2563m, it hardly requires a pre-dawn approach from the refuge. Nor are ropes, karabiners or climbing experience necessary. Luckily for 'mere' walkers, it's a short stroll due north from the hut. This isolated hillock is both a superb lookout and the highest point on the Sciliar massif. From here, you can admire the Sassopiatto–Sassolungo group to the east, the Catinaccio and its amazing towers to the south-east, then the majestic Latemar in the south.

Onward routes

❶ To turn a visit into a superb 2-day circuit, a recommended option is to ramble over the top of the Sciliar platform to the Denti di Terrarossa (translated as 'red earth teeth'). But it needs to be taken slowly so as not to miss the fascinating patches of fossilised coral en route. After dropping over the awesome Buco dell'Orso (bear's hole), a broad valley leads to the fire-red Rifugio Alpe di Tires at 2440m. From there, it's onward via Forcella Denti di Terrarossa before a return across the Alpe di Siusi meadows to Compaccio.

❷ Paths from Rifugio Alpe di Tires also link south into the awesome Catinaccio and its host of huts, as well as eastwards over to the Sassopiatto–Sassolungo formation.

Hut essentials

Location
Bernese Alps, Switzerland

Valley base
Fiesch

Hut capacity
32 places

Staffed
from June to mid October

Tel
+41 (0)27 971 40 27

Website
www.burghuette.ch

Guidebooks
Walking in the Valais and *100 Hut Walks in the Alps* (Cicerone Press); *Bernese Oberland* (Alpine Club)

Set among a scattering of larch and pine trees overlooking the deep gorge of the once mighty Fiescher glacier, the privately owned Burg Hut does not look directly onto any great mountains, but it only takes a short walk or cable-assisted scramble up the slabs behind it to enjoy a truly spectacular view. Beyond a thinning screen of trees, far to the south across the Rhône Valley, a glimpse may be had of the eastern Pennine Alps brushing against the Lepontines. But to the north – ah, now, that's something special, for the glacier gorge is headed by the eye-catching wall of abrupt, challenging peaks of the Fiescherhörner, which will surely set

any climber's fingers itching. Bursting from modest ribbons of snow and ice, it's a scene of rock upon rock, intimidating or inviting – take your pick. But if rock climbing is your forte, there's no need to spend the next few hours working your way into what appears to be the very heart of the Bernese Alps, because the ridge on which the hut has been built falls in a series of easy-to-access slabs, adopted as a popular *Klettergarten* or practice area for climbers, with routes from 120–200 metres in length. The standard approach route to the hut passes along its base.

Built of stone and heavy, dark-weathered timbers, the Burg Hut has a panelled *Stube* (dining room) adorned with framed photographs and items of old climbing equipment, and a small balcony outside, where, as evening settles over the mountains, you can sit with a drink after a hard day in the hills and wait for dinner to be served. Dormitories

'the whole place exudes an air of gentle cosiness, as though the world outside is resting'

are small, old-fashioned *Lager* (mattress rooms), and washing facilities are pretty

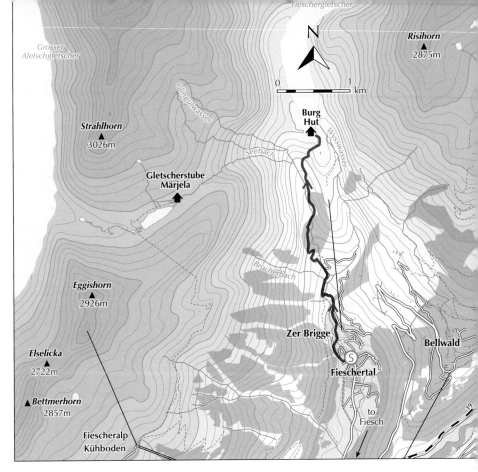

basic, but the whole place exudes an air of gentle cosiness, as though the world outside is resting. And the walk to it is, quite simply, lovely.

Having twice walked up to the hut from Fiesch and returned the same day, it was good to spend a night there as part of a longer tour. This time, my daughter was with me. It was her first alpine hut and a perfect one for her initiation. The place was less than half full and we shared a dormitory with a Swiss couple who expressed a natural pride in 'their' mountains. Since they'd just descended the route we planned to take next day,

and we had approached by the way they intended to go, trail information was traded across the table as we ate, after which discussions ranged across a dozen different subjects and continued until lights-out, then resumed over breakfast next morning. As has happened so many times in so many huts, a common need had brought strangers together and turned them into friends.

Approach route

The Fieschertal is the longest of the northern tributaries to spill out of the Bernese Alps into the Goms – the upper reaches of the Rhône's valley – with the modest little resort of Fiesch at its entrance. From here, a bus runs upvalley to the roadhead at **Fieschertal** Dorfplatz bus stop, where the 2–2½-hour approach walk begins on a gravel track between meadows. After passing a group of dark-timbered chalets and old hay barns at **Zer Brigge**, a footpath continues, leap-frogging a service road for a while, then among sparse woods and glades of moss-covered rocks overhung by rowan and wild raspberry canes. You come to rough meadows where scattered boulders are studded with scarlet-headed houseleek; there's a solitary herdsman's hut and a stream in which to cool sun-burned arms on a hot summer's day.

Turn right at a trail junction at 1573m and wander into a mini-gorge (or broad gully), whose enticing slabs on both sides form part of the *Klettergarten*. As you clamber up the narrowing slope to a short iron ladder at its head, climbers are bound to be at work on either side or high above you. From the top of the ladder you turn left, and moments later discover the welcome sight of the **Burg Hut** just ahead, and a stomach-churning surprise drop on the right into the depths of the now ice-free glacier gorge.

Onward routes

❶ A favoured return route to the Fieschertal departs back along the ridge on which the hut is set and crosses the head of the mini-gorge up which the approach walk came. After climbing and descending other metal ladders bolted to more rock slabs, it descends among trees and small open meadows with fine views most of the way (1½ hours to Fieschertal Dorfplatz).

❷ A steep but rewarding route takes the mountain walker above the hut heading roughly north-west to gain a high plateau slung between mountains on the edge of the Grosser Aletschgletscher – the longest icefield in the Alps. The route begins by climbing slabs immediately above the hut, using a fixed cable for aid.

The attractive, privately owned stone- and timber-built Burg Hut is a very special place to spend a night or two

The panelled Stube at the Burg Hut helps create a cosy atmosphere

dotted with tiny lakes. Here, you'll find another privately owned hut, the Gletscherstube Märjela (2373m), about 2½ hours from the Burg Hut. The Aletschgletscher is just a few minutes' walk from here.

Ascents

Most high peaks are too far away for the Burg Hut to be used as a base, but the twin Wannenzwillinge (3481m and 3432m) and Klein Wannenhorn (3707m) offer rock climbs in a high mountain setting.

It then twists among trees before joining a clear path that soon swings left on a rising traverse of a steep grass slope, eventually spilling out onto level pastures

Striped with moraine, the Grosser Aletschgletscher makes a long and gradual descent from Konkordiaplatz

Cabane des Dix (2928m)

Hut essentials

Location
Pennine Alps, Switzerland

Valley base
Arolla

Hut capacity
120 places

Staffed
from mid March to mid May, and late June to late September

Tel
+41 (0)27 281 15 23

Website
www.cabanedesdix.ch

Guidebooks
Walking in the Valais, Chamonix to Zermatt: The Classic Walker's Haute Route and *100 Hut Walks in the Alps* (Cicerone Press); *Valais Alps West* (Alpine Club)

Built in 1908, the Dix Hut sits on a plug of rock with a direct, full frontal view of Mont Blanc de Cheilon's great triangular wedge of a north face. Easing from the base of the mountain, the stone-pitted ice of the Cheilon glacier takes on the role of grey moat to the hut's rocky fortress, its outflowing torrent pouring through a wild genesis-like valley before emptying (out of sight from the hut) into Lac des Dix, whose immense barrage appears from below to block the head of Val d'Hérémence. On the eastern side of the dividing ridge flanking the glacier, and several hours' walk away, Arolla nestles among pinewood and pasture, a resort

modest in all but its reputation among climbers, ski mountaineers and Haute Route trekkers, whose numbers have helped turn Cabane des Dix into one of the most popular of all huts owned by the Swiss Alpine Club (Schweizer Alpen-Club, SAC).

I remember one occasion when a long day and a heavy rucksack slowed my approach from the Val d'Hérémence, so a first sighting of the hut as I crossed a shoulder of the Tête Noire came as a great relief. Another 10 minutes – give or take – and I'd be there. Trouble is, the very last few metres are up a steeply climbing path and my legs had turned to lead. Bad timing! Suddenly the guardian appeared, waving his arms and calling for me to hurry. Hurry? It's all I could do to put one foot in front of the other. I was exhausted. 'Quick, quick,' he seemed to be shouting, 'ze helicopter is coming!' A helicopter? Yes, the helicopter that brings supplies to the hut. It was about to come zooming over the ridge from Arolla, then over the glacier before making a circuit of the hut with a great net of food supplies hanging from it. And I was in the way.

It was all I could do to breathe, let alone hurry. So the guardian raced down the slope, tore the rucksack from my shoulders and scurried back up the slope with it under one arm. Unburdened, I found a modicum of strength and, with what seemed like my last breath, just reached the hut terrace when the

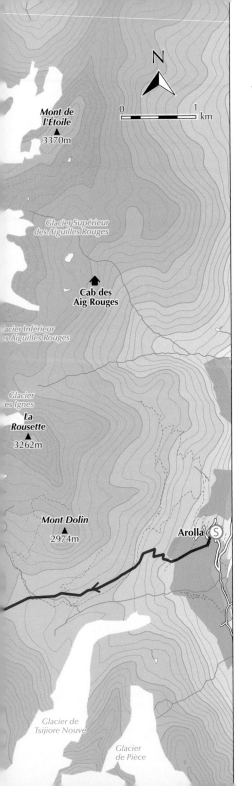

whirlybird arrived in a frantic battery of noise, whipping hats from heads and creating wild spirals of dust. It took 10 minutes before my heart stopped thrashing...

When busy, Cabane des Dix has a friendly buzz to it; there's enough staff to handle the throng of climbers and trekkers in need of food and drink after a full day's activity, and the dining room looks out at a wild scene – dormitories likewise – although in common with so many huts in challenging locations, the washroom and 'environmental' toilet facilities are, well, somewhat limited, but understandably so.

Distant from everything, once night falls Cabane des Dix seems to be lodged among the stars, lost in a silent world of

> 'once night falls Cabane des Dix seems to be lodged among the stars, lost in a silent world of its own'

its own – until, that is, the pre-dawn creak and thump of heavy feet tells of climbers making their way to breakfast, leaving trekkers to their blankets for another couple of hours or more. There's plenty to climb around here, and the view from the hut terrace reveals an amphitheatre of peaks from which to choose: Rosablanche,

La Salle, Le Pleureur, La Luette, Mont Blanc de Cheilon, Pigne d'Arolla and the ragged Aiguilles Rouges. These may not be summits on the list of top-grade climbers, but they have lots of appeal for a first alpine season.

Approach routes

① From the road above the village square in **Arolla**, the way to the Dix Hut takes a track through woods of Arolla pine leading to the Grand Hotel Kurhaus. Thereafter, a path continues among trees, but when these give way to rolling pastures, views open to reveal Mont Collon, Pigne d'Arolla and glacial highways flanked by long moraine walls. The path gives onto a farm track, but after crossing a stream, you revert to a mountain path heading up to a secluded basin of boulder-strewn grass.

The way forks at the foot of the ridge beyond which lies Val des Dix. The left-hand trail climbs to the 2855m **Pas de Chèvres**, while the alternative makes for

Standing on its plug of rock, Cabane des Dix is one of the busiest of all Swiss huts

the **Col de Riedmatten** at 2919m. Both crossings lead to the hut; Pas de Chèvres descends via a stairway of ladders, the narrow Col de Riedmatten provides a steep descent on unstable grit. Both give stunning views back to Mont Collon and the distant tip of the Matterhorn, and ahead to Mont Blanc de Cheilon. The two routes come together on the edge of the **Cheilon glacier**, which you then cross directly to the rocky knoll on which stands **Cabane des Dix** (4–4½ hours from Arolla).

② A shorter route in terms of walking time (3–3½ hours) and a more direct approach begins at **Le Chargeur** at the Val d'Hérémence roadhead, where a steep path (*téléphérique*/cable car option) climbs to the top of the massive dam wall. From here, a track entices along the west side of **Lac des Dix**, initially through a series of tunnels, then beside pastures loud with the sound of cowbells. From the southern end of the lake, a signed path rises along the moraine bank of the Cheilon glacier, with views growing wilder and more impressive across the valley as you progress towards the minor rock peak of the **Tête Noire**. Skirting this on its western side, you cross a shoulder of the Tête and gain a first sighting of the hut which, from a distance, is reminiscent of a toy-sized medieval castle, dwarfed by Mont Blanc de Cheilon. The path drops into a little glacial plain, then climbs the slope leading directly to **Cabane des Dix**.

Ascents

Mont Blanc de Cheilon (3869m) is a natural lure, its normal route of ascent often visited on a traverse to the Pigne d'Arolla, while its classic north face is, in summer, now pure rock, having lost the sheen of ice and snow that previously added much to its appeal. Springtime ski ascents are also popular; and in summer, trekkers following the Chamonix to Zermatt Walker's Haute Route skirt the base of the mountains when they visit Cabane des Dix on the way from Prafleuri to Arolla.

Refuge Entre Deux Eaux (2120m)

Hut essentials

Location
Graian Alps, France

Valley base
Termignon

Hut capacity
38 places

Staffed
from June to end of September

Tel
+33 (0)4 79 05 27 13

Website
www.refugeentredeuxeaux.com

Guidebooks
Tour of the Vanoise **and** ***100 Hut Walks in the Alps (Cicerone* Press)**

The heart of the Vanoise National Park is crowned by the 3855m Grande Casse and its 'twin', the Grande Motte, set upon a connecting ridge to the east but some 200m lower than its big brother at 3651m. The south face of the Grande Casse erupts from an apron of scree and well-watered grass where Vallon de la Leisse swings south towards the Doron gorge. At its foot there's a 16th-century stone bridge, and nearby, on the east flank of the valley just above the confluence of the Leisse and Rocheure rivers, stands the 100-year-old dairy farm of Entre Deux Eaux. In 1935, the Scottish climber Janet Adam Smith arrived here with her husband, the climber and poet Michael Roberts. 'It was a whitewashed stone chalet', she wrote, in her book *Mountain Holidays*, 'rather like a farmhouse in the Lakes, long and low, rising at one end to a second storey.' She learned that the family who lived there 'came up with the cows every summer [and] put up climbers or walkers…usually two or three parties every night,' and described with relish that her dinner was delicious: 'broth, bacon and eggs, French beans, salad, *crème fraîche* and quince jam, and an admirable *vin rosé*.'

Although a number of huts within the national park belong to either the French Alpine Club (Fédération Française des Clubs Alpins et de Montagne, FFCAM) or the park authority, Refuge Entre Deux Eaux is privately owned, and Janet Adam Smith's description remains true more than 80 years after she wrote of it. What's more, the welcome she received in 1935 is just as warm today. The building has character, it's cosy and comfortable, and although its location is perhaps a little too distant from the high peaks to make it a perfect base from which to climb some of the best routes of the district, its outlook is splendid and the walking first rate. Trekkers making a traverse of the region on either GR55 or GR5 pass close by, as do those tackling the Tour of the Vanoise.

It's easy to get to, a factor that makes it especially attractive for day visitors, but like so many alpine refuges, it's when the last passers-by have gone and evening

The village Entre Deux Eaux was once a dairy farm

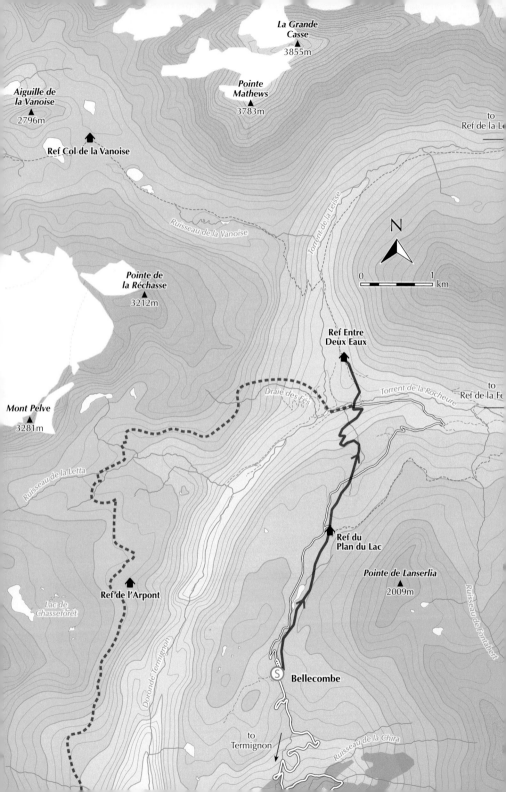

La Grande
Casse
3855m

Aiguille de
la Vanoise
2796m

Pointe
Mathews
3783m

Ref Col de la Vanoise

to
Ref de la L

Ruisseau de la Vanoise

Torrent de la Leïse

N

0   1 km

Pointe de
la Réchasse
3212m

Ref Entre
Deux Eaux

Draie des Fés

Torrent de la Rocheure

to
Ref de la Fe

Mont Pelve
3281m

Ruisseau de la Letta

Ref du
Plan du Lac

Pointe de Lanserlia
2009m

Ruisseau de Pontabert

Ref de l'Arpont

Lac de
Chasseforêt

Doron de Termignon

S Bellecombe

Ruisseau de la Chira

to
Termignon

settles over the hills that the real ambience of the place takes over. The sounds of an accordion or guitar might briefly fill the empty spaces, and dawn be greeted by a cock crowing, yet these are short-lived intrusions into what is otherwise the welcome peace of the mountains. Entre Deux Eaux somehow manages to create its own unique atmosphere of relaxation.

At least, that's what Min and I experienced when trekking the Tour of the Vanoise in the early summer of 1995. We'd come down from La Leisse, and with a day in hand, left our rucksacks at Entre Deux Eaux and went wandering into the nearby Vallon de la Rocheure before returning to the old farm-cum-refuge in the late afternoon. Hens clucked around us. Voices spoke softly. An air of calm seemed to emanate from every room. It was as though even the mountains held their breath. We could have stayed for a month.

Approach route

A glance at the map would rightly suggest a longish walk from Termignon, the nearest village in the Maurienne, the valley of l'Arc, which effectively forms the southern limits of the Parc National de la Vanoise (PNV). But a narrow twisting road climbs towards the mountains, pushing high above the east bank of the Doron gorge as far as a parking area known as **Bellecombe** at 2307m.

This is as far as private vehicles are permitted, but a shuttle bus continues to

the modern PNV-owned **Refuge du Plan du Lac**, a little north of an idyllic lake that gives wonderful reflected views of the mountains. Beyond the refuge, the shuttle crosses a modest col and descends to a bridge spanning the Torrent de la Rocheure, where it terminates. **Refuge Entre Deux Eaux** can be reached from here by a walk of only 15–20 minutes after crossing the bridge.

'It was as though even the mountains held their breath'

A longer and more satisfying approach walk (1½–2 hours) comes from the Bellecombe car park and follows a clear mountain trail nearly all the way.

Neighbouring huts

❶ Owned by the national park authority, Refuge de la Femma stands at 2323m near the head of the pastoral Vallon de la Rocheure cutting to the east of Entre Deux Eaux. It's a three-storey timber building reached by a walk of about 2 hours on a combination of old farm track and footpath. Almost 600m above the hut, Col de la Rocheure offers spectacular views, and is worth adding to your itinerary.

❷ Another PNV hut easily accessible from Entre Deux Eaux by a walk of about 2½ hours is Refuge de la Leisse – three

The idyllic Plan du Lac is visited on the approach to Entre Deux Eaux

wooden buildings with steeply-pitched roofs overlooking the lower Vallon de la Leisse from a spur of land 300m below Col de la Leisse. Used by trekkers on the Tour of the Vanoise, it's often very busy during the high summer season, but is a great place from which to observe marmot, chamois and ibex (*bouquetin*)

in the early mornings. Heading north from Entre Deux Eaux, the way into the Leisse valley curves right at the old Pont de Croé-Vie and leads directly to the hut, which is seen long before you reach it.
❸ As the name implies, the large and rather ugly three-building complex of Refuge du Col de la Vanoise stands on

the almost-level col north-west of Entre Deux Eaux at 2517m. Also known as Refuge Félix Faure after the French president who came here in 1897, it has 148 dorm places and is the property of the FFCAM. Views include the Grande Casse, Pointe de la Grande Glière and the impressive Aiguille de l'Épéna. A 2-hour walk from Entre Deux Eaux is all that's needed to reach it, and the way is obvious once you've crossed the Pont de Croé-Vie, for a zigzag path climbs directly to the col, passing a triangular memorial stone, an old wartime gun-emplacement bunker and a series of shallow tarns on the way.

Hut essentials

Location
Kaisergebirge, Austria

Valley base
Ellmau

Hut capacity
150 places

Staffed
from June to mid October

Tel
+43 (0)5358 43389

Website
www.grutten-huette.at

Guidebooks
Walking in Austria and ***100 Hut Walks in the Alps*** (Cicerone Press)

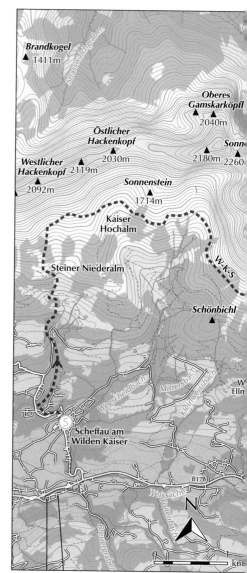

The Kaisergebirge is the compact range of limestone peaks on which the great Austrian mountaineer Hermann Buhl cut his teeth as a rock climber. But he was just one of many to be drawn to the dramatic walls bursting from the gentle combination of pasture and forest that surround them, and every day in summer the sound of climbers at work with their jangling ironmongery echoes from crag to crag. 'From every route, wall, *arête*, gully, crack and chimney you could hear the exchange of climbers' talk,' wrote Buhl in *Nanga Parbat Pilgrimage*. 'From opposite, the climbers looked like tiny flies on sky-raking walls.' There are via ferrata routes too (known as *Klettersteig* here), while at the base of the mountains wind a number of well-marked and well-walked trails. No fewer than nine huts

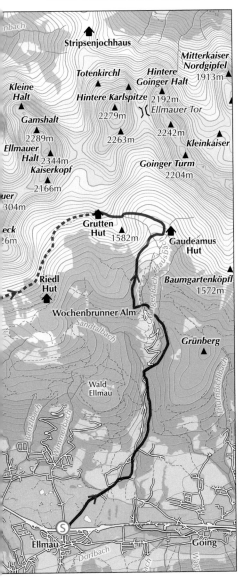

service the area, with the Grutten Hut being one of the largest.

It stands on a grassy terrace projecting from the foot of Ellmauer Halt, highest of the Kaisergebirge summits, with a view south across the green Kitzbüheler Alps to the distant Grossvenediger, and east to the ragged tops of the continuing wall of the Wilder Kaiser. Easily reached by a direct walk of no more than an hour from the roadhead, it is understandably busy with day visitors, many of whom do little more than sit on the terrace with a

'Never was an ice-cold beer more welcome, nor the joyful chatter of climbers discussing their day's exploits'

plate of schnitzel and a foaming tankard of beer as they enjoy the outlook across the valley. But at night, the *Stube* (common room) is full of climbers' talk, and walkers discussing the day's activities. Peace envelopes the soaring crags outside, and the valley below is a mass of twinkling lights.

Work had taken me to the Kaisergebirge on a number of occasions, and I'd often stopped at the Grutten Hut for refreshment. But it wasn't until I made a

Backed by the crags of the Wilder Kaiser mountains, the Grutten Hut looks out towards the more modest Kitzbüheler Alps

multi-day tour of the district in the summer of 2007 that I had an opportunity to spend a night there (see Tour of the Wilder Kaiser in Chapter 4). It happened to be one of the hottest days of the year when I'd set off from the bustling Stripsenjochhaus on the northern side of the range, and before long I was bathed in sweat as I worked my way alone up the Eggersteig – one of the earliest of all *Klettersteig* routes – towards the huge cleft of Ellmauer Tor. Hours later, I emerged through that 'gateway' with its far-reaching views, and descended a furnace of scree before getting onto the next *Klettersteig* route, the classic Jubilaumssteig with all its pinnacles, turrets and towers, which eventually ejected me onto soft grass just a few minutes' walk from the Grutten Hut. Never was an ice-cold beer

more welcome, nor the joyful chatter of climbers discussing their day's exploits on the terrace as the sun went down. And for once my fellow guests at the hut allowed the dorm windows to remain open throughout the night, allowing some cool, fresh air to circulate. And that had to be a first!

The hut is comfortable and well-run. There are 50 beds in family rooms, and 100 dormitory places. Built in 1899, it has been extended several times since then, and the facilities are among the best to be found hereabouts.

Approach routes

❶ The obvious approach comes directly from the attractive little resort of **Ellmau**, one of the nicest of the tourist villages that lie at the foot of the Wilder Kaiser (the higher and more southerly of the two parallel ridges of the Kaisergebirge range). It is possible to drive as far as the **Wochenbrunner Alm**, from where a clear stony path rises via the **Gaudeamus Hut** to the **Grutten Hut** in 1–1½ hours, while to walk all the way from Ellmau would add another 1½ hours.

❷ **Scheffau**, one of Ellmau's neighbouring villages, gives a longer and more interesting route of approach (4 hours) on a section of the Wilder-Kaiser-Steig (WKS) – a 35km trail that runs along the southern flank of the mountains. This is gained above the steep pastures of the **Steiner Niederalm**, about 1½ hours from Scheffau.

Once on the WKS, yellow-and-black waymarks guide the route through beech woods and out to a scene of wild craggy mountains, with the buildings of **Kaiser Hochalm** nestling in their shadow. The way continues in and out of woods, across screes and on a steep flight of steps hewn from the rock; it's an undulating course with views of the Kitzbüheler Alps in one direction, and the soaring slabs and pinnacles of the Kaisergebirge looming overhead. About 3½ hours from Scheffau the trail forks. The right branch descends to the small, privately-owned **Riedl Hut**, while the upper trail continues on the WKS for another 30 minutes to reach the **Grutten Hut**.

Ascents

There's no shortage of climbs to be made from a base here. Ellmauer Halt (2344m), rising directly behind the hut, is an obvious attraction, the standard route taking about 3 hours. The Kleine Halt, Treffauer, Karlspitzen and Goinger Halt are all accessible. A number of the most famous Kaisergebirge rock routes on the Fleischbank, Predigstuhl and Totenkirchl can also be reached from the Grutten Hut, although the Stripsenjochhaus, located on the northern side of the range, is more popular for these. A classic *Klettersteig* route, the Jubilaumssteig, is only a few minutes' walk away, and is used by climbers (and walkers) making their way up to or from the massive 'gateway' of Ellmauer Tor.

Onward routes

❶ Beginning near Kirchdorf, the Wilder-Kaiser-Steig (mentioned as part of the approach to the hut from Scheffau), makes a 2-day east–west traverse of the Wilder Kaiser's south flank, ending at Kufstein. The Grutten Hut is the preferred option for an overnight stay midway along the route. As it sits roughly at the halfway point, a day's walk in either direction is worth considering.

❷ A crossing of the range through the well-known cleft of Ellmauer Tor makes an excellent, if challenging, day out for experienced walkers. Enlivened by such *Klettersteig* routes as the Jubilaumssteig and Eggersteig, the crossing ends either at the Stripsenjochhaus (a large hut perched on a 'cross-bar' of a ridge that connects the Wilder and Zahmer Kaiser mountains) or at Griesner Alm in the lovely Kaiserbachtal.

Hut essentials

Location
Bernina Alps, Italy

Valley base
Chiesa or Chiareggio

Hut capacity
32 places

Staffed
from June to mid September

Tel
+39 0342 451120

Website
www.rifugi.lombardia.it

Guidebooks
Tour of the Bernina and *100 Hut Walks in the Alps* (Cicerone Press); *Bernina and Bregaglia* (Alpine Club)

goni, located below the cliffs that support what's left of the lower Scerscen glacier.

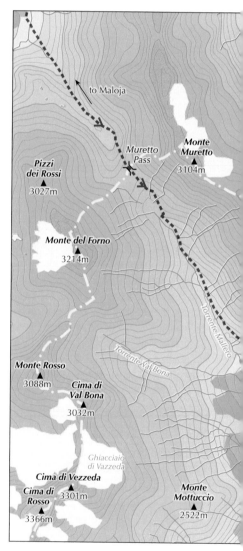

Cutting a swathe through the mountains roughly north of Sondrio in Valtellina, Val Malenco separates the Bregaglia Alps from the Bernina. Truly alpine at its head, with snow and ice-crowned peaks on either side, the lower valley spills out to vineyards and orchards and the bright light of Lombardy. Halfway up the valley, and reached by bus from Sondrio, Chiesa, the main township of Val Malenco, spreads along tiers on the west flank, while at the roadhead below the Muretto Pass stands Chiareggio, a small one-street village that makes a decent base for a few days of a walking or climbing holiday. One of the finest outings from here leads to Rifugio Lon-

Understandably popular with local walkers, with climbers on their way to tackle routes on the south flank of the Bernina massif, and with trekkers fol-

lowing either the Tour of the Bernina or the 8-day Alta Via Valmalenco, Rifugio Longoni is an old-fashioned hut whose wood-burning stove throws its generous

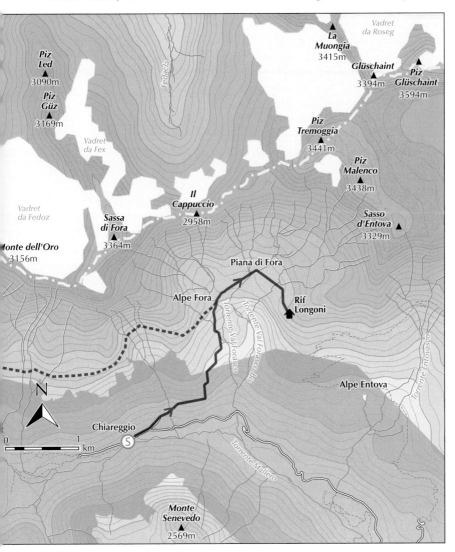

heat across the communal dining room – especially welcome when a raw wind hammers at the windows. Located about 850m above Chiareggio on the steep north side of Val Malenco, it has a tremendous view from the terrace towards Monte Disgrazia seen across the valley to the south, and south-east to Lago Palù beside which there's another *rifugio*. The Longoni hut was built in 1938 and the current *gestore* (warden) has managed the place for over 20 years. Facilities are modest, with 32 places in dormitories on two floors, but it has showers, the meals

> 'when clouds sank low and a cool wind scoured the hillside, we gathered round the stove and wallowed in its heat'

are excellent and the building is imbued with a cosy atmosphere.

I found my way there on a summer's day in the mid 1990s when on research in the Italian Alps for a major writing project. At the time I had a tight schedule to maintain, which left no quality time to spend at the hut – a great pity, for its location and ambience were enough to make me regret having to move on. But two decades later I was back, this time

making the Tour of the Bernina with Jonathan, my publisher. He had more puff than I and arrived at the *rifugio* an hour or so ahead of me. Well, I was dawdling to study the flowers and waterfalls (that was my excuse), while the *gestore* apparently scanned the hillside through binoculars to check that I was still moving! Even so, I was there early enough to enjoy a bowl of hot soup for lunch, and when clouds sank low and a cool wind scoured the hillside, we gathered round the stove and wallowed in its heat. Apart from the *gestore* and his son, we had the place to ourselves, and spent the rest of the day and evening planning our route with advice from our host, a professional guide who knew every peak, hill and hollow with an intimacy only possible for those who live among the high places. That knowledge and advice, along with his culinary skills, made our stay at Rifugio Longoni one to remember.

Approach routes

❶ The reasonably short but beautiful 2½-hour walk from **Chiareggio** is a classic of its kind. It begins at the downvalley end of the village, where a track rises easily between drystone walls to a group of old stone buildings that go by the name of La Corte. Leaving the track, a path climbs steep wooded slopes for about 400m to reach **Alpe Fora**, from where you gain a sublime view of Monte Disgrazia. The way continues to climb in order to reach the wonderful flowery shelf of **Piana di Fora**. Running with streams, the shelf, or

...gio Longoni is a delightfully old-fashioned hut lodged high above Val Malenco

marshy basin, is backed by cliffs striped by a number of photogenic waterfalls. Nearby, there's a stone-built hut (locked), a small lake and yet more fine views. After crossing the basin, you wander up a series of glacier-smoothed slabs to gain a high point at 2455m, from where **Rifugio Longoni** is just 5 minutes away.

❷ Trekkers following the Tour of the Bernina approach the hut from Maloja on a 7½–8-hour stage that crosses into Italy at the 2562m **Muretto Pass**, then traverses round the east flank of Val Malenco before joining the Chiareggio trail at **Alpe Fora**.

Onward routes

❶ Both the Tour of the Bernina and Alta Via Valmalenco continue their circuits by heading south-eastward to Lago Palù, a pine-ringed lake at 1947m overlooked by another *rifugio* (more hotel than refuge) with a well-patronised restaurant.

There are two options: the standard route remains 'high' and takes about 4½ hours, while the lower and slightly easier variant should be achievable in a little over 3 hours. Both start by descending from Rifugio Longoni to a track, although anyone attempting to reach the

A wood-burning stove throws its warmth across the Longoni Stube

track by the so-called shortcut heading east from the hut is likely to regret the effort involved. Take the easy option and drop down to the track where, soon after, there's a parting of the ways. The main route remains high, while the alternative forks right and then takes a path to Alpe Entova, joining a farm track to the buildings of Braciascia. Here, another path breaks away to Il Barchetto and Lago Palù.

❷ A much more demanding route than the two options offered for Lago Palù and its *rifugio* sets out on a stiff 5-hour trek to Rifugio Marinelli Bombardieri, a large mountaineer's hut lodged below the Scerscen and Caspoggio glaciers at 2813m – allow 5 hours at least for this.

Ascents

The hut's location makes several climbs possible on the Bernina massif's various summits; among them Sassa di Fora, Piz Tremoggia, Piz Malenco, Sassa d'Entova and Piz Glüschaint. The hut warden can advise.

Totalp Hut (2385)

As with many huts, it's the Totalp's location that makes it extra special. The 'dead alp' from which it draws its name is a stony wilderness caught among the lower slopes of the Schesaplana, highest of the Rätikon mountains at 2964m. A hollow just below the hut contains a small lake, but you only need to walk a few paces in the other direction to look down on the turquoise expanse of the Lünersee, and above that cast your eye along the backbone of mountains that forms the Austrian–Swiss border, where the Kirchlispitzen dominates. The Rätikon Alps are not snowy alps, except in winter. They're bold and craggy limestone struc-

Hut essentials

Location
Rätikon Alps, Austria

Valley base
Brand

Hut capacity
85 places

Staffed
from June to early October

Tel
+43 (0)664 2400 260

Website
www.totalp.at

Guidebooks
Walking in Austria and *Trekking in the Silvretta and Rätikon Alps* (Cicerone Press)

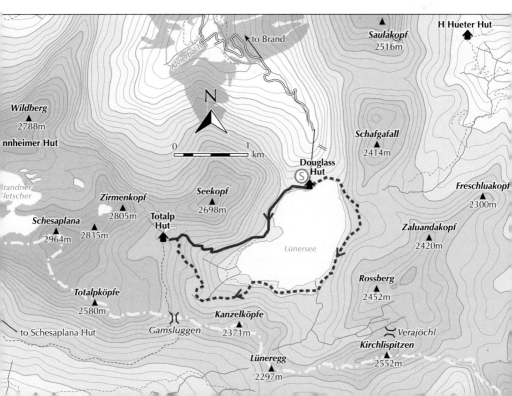

'Dead alp' is an apt name for the stony wilderness on which the Totalp Hut is set, but it's a welcoming place for all that

tures, lacking the glaciers and altitude of the Western Alps but no less beautiful for being modest in height. They rise above screes and meadows rich in alpine plants, and while their walls seduce climbers with numerous challenging routes, the trails that skirt their ankles and cross the passes that divide them offer some of the finest hut-to-hut routes of the Eastern Alps. The Totalp Hut is used not only by climbers drawn to the Schesaplana but also by day walkers based in Brand,

shelter than the large timber construction that houses 85 in its dormitories today. The present hut dates from 1974 and is a bustling place in the high season – although most of those who call there are passing visitors making the straightforward ascent of the Schesaplana and returning to a valley base at the end of the day. Those who stay the night will find the facilities adequate, bunk beds comfortable and the meals filling and tasty. And if you're there with a full moon in the sky, you'll no doubt be enchanted by the scene outside.

My first visit followed a bivouac in a meadow above Brand, and arriving at the hut in time for a late breakfast I left my rucksack with the guardian, made my ascent of the Schesaplana and was back down in time for lunch and an afternoon snoozing in the sunshine. A Nepalese Sherpa was working there, and when his duties allowed, we swapped stories about his home mountains, reminiscing about the valleys and villages, and a number of treks we had both made in the Khumbu. Summer being monsoon time in the Himalaya, he told me that each year he escapes the rain and the leeches of the Nepalese mountains and comes to Austria for a few months' employment in the Alps. 'Good here,' he

and by trekkers straying from the Rätikon Höhenweg.

Owned by the Vorarlberg section of the Austrian Alpine Club (Österreichischer Alpenverein, ÖAV), the original hut, built in 1964, was a much more modest

told me. 'Good as Nepal. Mountains not so high, but I like.' He indicated the view to the frontier mountains, then nodded down towards the lake. 'I like,' he repeated.

Me too.

Approach route

The standard route of approach is through the Brandnertal, which reaches into the mountains from Bludenz. Brand is the mid-valley resort that makes the most convenient base. From there, a bus runs south as far as a cable car station below the barrage wall of the Lünersee reservoir. The upper cable car station is on the crest of the barrage beside the **Douglass Hut**.

From here, there are two options. For the shorter route, take the track that cuts along the west bank of the **Lünersee** for about 15 minutes, then follow a signed path rising across the slopes of the **Seekopf** all the way to the **Totalp Hut** (1½ hours from the Douglass Hut).

Alternatively, cross the reservoir barrage past the **Douglass Hut** to join a path running along the east bank of the lake. On reaching the southern end, continue past the Lünersee Alm to a path junction near the base of the hut's goods lift. Cut left here and climb a grassy slope to join the west bank path, and follow this to the **Totalp Hut** (about 2½ hours from the Douglass Hut).

Ascent

The reason for the Totalp Hut's existence is to facilitate the ascent of the Schesaplana. Despite being the highest of the Rätikon Alps, under normal summer conditions the ascent from the hut is not difficult and the standard route is well marked for most of the way, demanding little more than 1½ hours via the east flank and south-west ridge.

Onward routes

❶ Trekkers following the splendid Rätikon Höhenweg make their way to the Lindauer Hut in about 4 hours, after first descending to the Lünersee Alm at the southern end of the Alm's eponymous lake, then heading roughly eastward over first the Verajöchl and then the Öfapass. From there, you make a fairly steep descent to the large Obere Sporaalpe with its classic view of the Drei Türme, shortly before arriving at the Lindauer Hut set among a stand of larch trees.

❷ A fine, if somewhat challenging, 2½-hour route linking the Totalp Hut with the Schesaplana Hut, on the Swiss side of the mountain, crosses the Gamsluggen – a narrow section of ridge, rather than a conventional pass, at 2378m. The way is signed from the Totalp Hut, with a series of waymarks and cairns that guide the way over low bands of rock and occasional patches of snow high above the Lünersee. Once over the ridge, fixed chains give support on steep and exposed slabs, before a zigzag descent on unstable ground leads to a welcome path cutting across pastures. Now, among banks of alpenrose and clutters of rock, the way leads directly to the Schesaplana Hut.

4 Hut to hut

These refuges may be basic, but they are functional, comfortable and well organised and provide good food, drink – pretty much all that a walker can desire – except perhaps a single room with en suite bathroom, Jacuzzi, newspaper, a glass of fine red wine and a piano.

(David Le Vay, *A Tour of Mont Blanc*)

Trekking from hut to hut has never been more popular than it is today, for many outdoor enthusiasts have discovered not just the joy of wandering day after day across the mountains, but also that 'hutting' is a sociable activity and a great way to make friends and discover exciting new areas. It's a very different experience from simply visiting a hut there-and-back from a valley base. Many multi-day routes enable you to stay at high altitude for days at a time

y 2 of the Tour of the Vanoise ends at the atmospheric Refuge de Plan Sec

Approaching the Rotstock Hut (Photo: Lesley Williams)

without descending to valleys and villages, so there's no interruption in the flow of your journey and you gain a closer relationship with a district – a better understanding of the lie of the land. There's often a series of passes to cross, with fresh panoramas to unravel; views that contain not only distant summits but all the natural features essential to the mountain landscape; and each hut you stay in will be different.

Here, listed in order of difficulty, is a small selection of multi-day hut routes that give plenty of variety and opportunities to gather a harvest of experiences. In order to give an idea of difficulty, I've graded them as follows:

- Moderate: 6–12 days of trekking on good paths, with a few fairly demanding ascents/descents
- Strenuous: up to 14 days, with some high or steep passes to cross – could include some exposed sections
- Demanding: 3–14 days, with a succession of high or steep passes, and occasional stretches of difficult and exposed terrain

Location	Graian Alps, France
Duration	10–12 days
Accommodation	Mountain huts, *gîtes d'étape* and hotels
Start/Finish	Modane in the Maurienne
Grade	Moderate
Guidebook	*Tour of the Vanoise* (Cicerone Press)

South of the Mont Blanc range, the Graian Alps spread across the French–Italian border – Vanoise Alps in France, Gran Paradiso in Italy. Not as high as either Mont Blanc and its satellite peaks or those of the Écrins to the south, the Vanoise region is nonetheless a seductive environment in which to wander. Making almost a figure-of-eight circuit of the Parc National de la Vanoise (PNV), this is a tour that would suit first-time trekkers. Although there are several passes to cross (the highest, Col de Chavière, being at 2796m), the physical demands are moderate, while the variety of huts and the distance between them makes each stage a pleasure. Many huts have been adapted from traditional farmhouses, the old mottled stone from which they were built blending into the landscape; they belong to the land. Around them, meadows are carpeted in early summer with an extravagant display of wildflowers, and there's abundant wildlife to be seen practically every day.

The first day involves a steep uphill trek through woodland to reach the comfortable **Refuge de l'Orgère**, a modern PNV-owned hut on a sloping meadow almost 900m above Modane. Thereafter, the route takes an undulating course along the Maurienne flank of the national park, crosses the grass saddle of Col du Barbier, curves into a deep combe below the Dent Parrachée and brings you to the quaintly hospitable **Refuge de Plan Sec**.

Day 3 is a little more demanding: it climbs to a 2363m saddle known as La Turra, and continues up for another 100m before entering a valley sliced by the Doron gorge, which threatens to cut the Vanoise region in two. At the head of the valley stands the district's highest summit, the snow-capped 3855m Grande Casse. It's an impressive mountain that appears to block the head of the valley with its massive wall of snow-plastered rock. On the way towards it, you pass one or two ruined farms and a series of lovely cascades. Ibex (*bouquetin*) can often be seen here, marmots too, their shrill warning cries mingling with the sound of crashing water as you make the final

approach to **Refuge de l'Arpont** – another reconstructed farm building.

Next day you continue towards the Grande Casse, but then drop into the head of the valley and cross to the east side below the charming **Refuge Entre Deux Eaux**. A climb of about 400m

'look back to capture one of the classic views of the whole tour'

then brings you to another PNV hut, the stone-built **Refuge du Plan du Lac**, from whose terrace splendid views draw your eyes over to the west side of the valley where glacial tongues lick distant summits, then north to the Grande Casse

once more. But this is best seen when you set out on the morning of Day 5, for within a few short minutes of leaving the hut, you pass alongside the beautiful lake after which the hut is named, and at its southern shore look back to capture one of the classic views of the whole tour, with the Grande Casse and Grande Motte turned on their heads in the water.

Days 5 and 6 return the trek to the valley of the Maurienne, Day 5 concluding at **Refuge de Vallonbrun**, and Day 6 bringing the walk down into the valley itself for a night at **Bonneval-sur-Arc**, one of the loveliest of old French mountain villages – a delight of medieval stone houses huddled at the foot of a steep slope, where accommodation is to be found in a *gîte*, a hotel, or an unmanned **CAF chalet-refuge**.

A relatively stiff 980m climb takes the route over the road pass of Col de l'Iseran

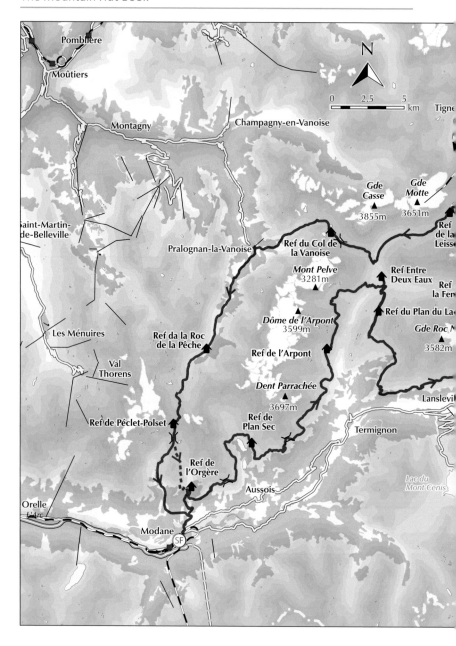

and down to **Val d'Isère** in the Tarentaise, for a night in a hotel and an opportunity to stock up with supplies for the second half of the trek. This second half quickly returns the route to the national park by way of the ski resort of Val Claret (an ugly high-rise intrusion, swiftly passed by), and the wild little pass of Col de la Leisse at 2758m. Once over this pass, the untamed nature of the Vanoise region offers a welcome return, with **Refuge de la Leisse** having a grandstand view of the unsullied valley into which you descend next day – a valley inhabited only by chamois and marmot.

Where the Vallon de la Leisse makes a sharp left-hand curve at the foot of the Grande Casse, the Tour of the Vanoise crosses the old arched bridge of Pont de Croé-Vie (only a stone's throw from the Entre Deux Eaux refuge) and begins the long twisting climb to Col de la Vanoise where there's yet another hut (**Refuge du Col de la Vanoise**, also known as Refuge Félix Faure). This is reached too soon to be of use if you've come directly from La Leisse, so you descend below big-walled crowding mountains on moraine and scree before using stepping stones to cross a shallow lake, and then continue a steepening descent to the township of **Pralognan-la-Vanoise**.

This leaves 2 days (3 days at the most) to return the trek to Modane, the first being a walk of about 14km through a steadily rising valley, with **Refuge de Péclet-Polset** your goal. Nestling among a bay of rugged mountains at 2474m, the

Stepping stones are used to cross Lac des Vaches after descending from Col de la Vanoise

refuge lies within striking distance of the last but highest of the trek's passes, the Col de Chavière, a little over 300m above the hut and gained by a rough walk over rocks that hide several little lakes and pools. Far-reaching views reward you at the pass, with the seductively ragged crests of the Écrins in one direction, Mont Blanc and Aiguille Noire in another. Then it's a long and steepish descent to **Modane**, with the option of diverting to **Refuge de l'Orgère** for a last night among mountains for those who, like me, wish to delay a return to 'civilisation' for as long as possible.

Rätikon Höhenweg

Location	Rätikon Alps, Switzerland, Austria and Liechtenstein
Duration	7–8 days
Accommodation	Mountain huts and hotels
Start/Finish	St Antönien (Switzerland) or Brand (Austria)
Grade	Moderate
Guidebook	*Trekking in the Silvretta and Rätikon Alps* (Cicerone Press)

Straddling the borders of three countries (Austria, Switzerland and tiny Liechtenstein), the Rätikon Alps are little known among the UK's mountaineering fraternity, yet these glorious limestone peaks are almost dolomitic in splendour – a rock climber's playground, but with summits accessible to most mountain walkers. A number of easy trails skirt their base, cross passes from one side of the international border to another, and link a host of charming traditional huts. On the Austrian side, the Rätikon Höhenweg Nord is a long-established linear hut-to-hut route, while the Rätikon Höhenweg Sud mimics its Austrian counterpart on the Swiss flank. By linking the two with a brief foray into Liechtenstein at the western end, and use of an easy grassy saddle at the eastern, a splendid figure-of-eight-shaped tour has been created.

Excellent public transport links with Zürich (flights from the UK) make the Rätikon accessible from three sides, but my preference for starting this particular trek is the attractive Swiss village of St Antönien above Kübris in the Prättigau valley, not far from the railway hub of Landquart – although Brand on the Austrian side is a good alternative.

The mountains are partly hidden from **St Antönien**, for the village nestles among rumpled hills, but it doesn't take long to rise above them to have the long blue-grey limestone Rätikon wall revealed, and since the first hut of the tour is not much more than a half day's walk away, there's time to enjoy the flowery pastures and lonely farms that inhabit the foothills. There's a small lake to visit too, before you turn a spur to gain a first view of the **Carschina Hut**, dwarfed at the foot of the bristling crags of the **Sulzfluh**. It's a fine hut with a big panorama to enjoy,

> 'It's a fine hut with a big panorama to enjoy'

and since it commands views to east and west, both sunrise and sunset can be spectacular.

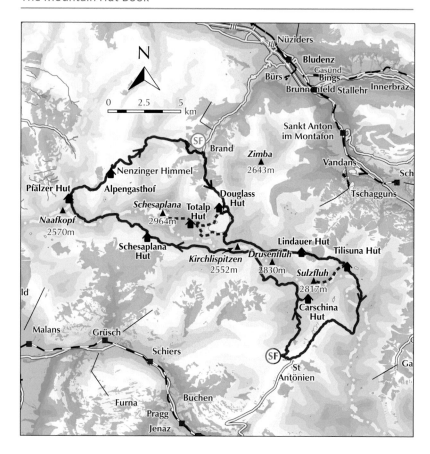

Leaving the Carschina Hut, a trail heads north-westward along the base of the majestic **Drusenfluh**, where a real bounty of alpine flowers spreads across the grassland, spills from beneath rocks and creates cushions on the screes. Passing below the cleft of the Schweizertor, a steep climb then takes you beside the towering **Kirchlispitzen**, on whose walls climbers appear not much larger than spiders. Topping a 2245m saddle at the west-ern end of the Kirchlispitzen's wall, the way drops into a region of rough pasture bordered by clumps of alpenrose to progress below more rock faces in view of the region's highest summit, the Schesaplana. At its foot stands the Schesaplana Hut, its back to the mountain, its face to the sun.

Day 3 is a delight of ever-changing vistas as you dodge from one country to another. It begins in Switzerland, strays into Liechtenstein and ends with a

descent into Austria. Immediately behind the Schesaplana Hut, a path makes
a traverse of the steep grassy slope that
falls away from crags forming the base
of the Schesaplana itself. The way then
climbs to the Klein Furgga to join the
Liechtensteinerweg across the flank of
the Hornspitz. Working round the headwall ridge of the Gamperdonatal you
then make for the **Naafkopf**, on whose
summit the three countries meet. Just
beyond this, built on a broad cross-
border saddle at 2108m, the **Pfälzer Hut**
is one of only two refuges belonging to
the Liechtenstein Alpine Club (Liechtensteiner Alpenverein, LAV). Unless you

wish to spend a night there, turn right
and descend into Austria, where overnight lodging can be found in the hamlet
of **Nenzinger Himmel**. Here, the large
Alpengasthof Gamperdona has modestly priced dormitory accommodation as
well as standard bedrooms, and enjoys
a peaceful location near the head of the
Gamperdonatal.

Next day, patches of forest and sloping pasture are linked by a trail that
climbs to the Amatschon Joch, a convenient crossing point on a grass ridge
separating the Gamperdonatal from the
Brandnertal. It's not a difficult crossing,
but I've always found the descent into

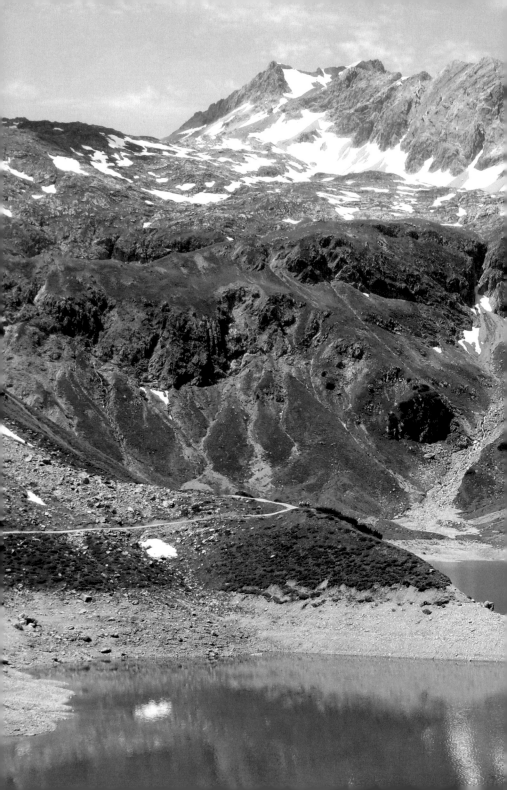

Schesaplana, highest of the Rätikon Alps, is clearly seen from the shores of the Lünersee. The Totalp Hut is on the rocky ledge above the grass

the Brandnertal to be tiring, despite a teasing view ahead to the lovely Zimba, one of the most distinctive of all Rätikon mountains. Once down in the valley bed, there is a choice: you could walk a short distance into the resort of **Brand** and catch a bus to the roadhead, where a cable car lifts weary trekkers to the Douglass Hut; or if you still have energy, head upvalley through more pasture and woodland close to the road, which brings you to the base of the Lünersee reservoir dam and the cableway. The large **Douglass Hut** is a noisy, busy place by day, but once the trippers have left it inspires a special atmosphere all its own.

> 'you can just make out the Lindauer Hut, snug in a grove of conifers 500m below'

Given sufficient time and energy, the ascent of the Schesaplana is a distinct possibility from here. The ascent route takes you round the western edge of the **Lünersee** and up past the splendid **Totalp Hut**. If this ascent appeals, it would be worth spending the night at the Totalp Hut following your climb, and next day join the continuing Rätikon Höhenweg on its way from the Douglass Hut to the Lindauer Hut. This traces the eastern side of the Lünersee before crossing two easy passes: the 2330m Verajöchl and the slightly lower Öfapass at 2291m. From the second of these you can just make out the Lindauer Hut, snug in a grove of conifers 500m below.

Dating from 1898 and largely rebuilt in 1956, the **Lindauer Hut** is a popular shingle-walled hut standing beside a celebrated botanical garden. The curious turrets of the Drei Türme erupt from the screes a short distance away.

The **Tilisuna Hut** is the next destination, for which a morning's walk is all that's needed. But having an afternoon spare, and given decent conditions, it would be worth leaving your rucksack at the hut and making the easy but worthwhile ascent of the **Sulzfluh** (2818m) – a route that crosses sections of limestone pavement and rewards you with extensive views from the summit.

The final stage of the trek leaves the Tilisuna Hut, heading roughly southward, and after an hour's easy walking brings you to the shallow Plasseggenpass at 2345m. From here, you descend into Switzerland through a great basin of pastureland to a funnel between cliffs, below which you wander among bleached limestone boulders, light-pink alpenrose and wonderful natural rock gardens on the way to Partnum. All that remains is to continue downvalley through more pastures and clumps of woodland to reach **St Antönien** for transport home.

Tour of the Jungfrau Region

Location	Bernese Alps, Switzerland
Duration	9–11 days
Accommodation	Mountain huts, inns and *Berghotels*
Start	Schynige Platte (above Wilderswil, near Interlaken)
Finish	Wilderswil
Grade	Moderate +
Guidebook	*Tour of the Jungfrau Region* (Cicerone Press)

Imagine sitting down to a meal with the iconic trio of Eiger, Mönch and Jungfrau gathering all the shades of alpenglow beyond your window, and in the morning when you wake, finding those same peaks riding a sea of cloud as the dawn light slips over the mountains. Such is the prospect from your first and last nights' accommodation on the Tour of the Jungfrau Region (TJR). And in between? Well, in between you wander day after day with a backdrop of yet more stately peaks: Wetterhorn, Schreckhorn, Finsteraarhorn, Fiescherhorn, Ebnefluh, Grosshorn, Breithorn, Tschingelhorn and Gspaltenhorn. And if that prospect fails to excite you, in the words of the great pre-war alpine connoisseur RLG Irving, 'you are better away from the Alps'.

The Tour of the Jungfrau Region makes a convoluted circuit, not around the elegant Jungfrau, but within the region over which it reigns, part of which has been named a UNESCO World Natural Heritage Site. With the deep gorge-like Lauterbrunnen Valley (that quintessential glacier-carved valley, streaming with waterfalls) dividing the trek into two distinct halves, accommodation on the way varies from hut to hotel, with some lovely old mountain inns too. While the trek itself crosses few passes, it does have some demanding sections, including the ascent of a 2970m mountain and one or two extremely steep descents.

It begins with a lazy ascent by way of a century-old cog railway from **Wilderswil**, at 584m, to **Schynige Platte** at 1980m, where a celebrated *Berghotel* makes an ideal overnight stop before setting out on the trek. Of course, you could start the tour as soon as you leave the train, but the magical panoramic view from the *Berghotel*, just a short stroll above the station, combined with the prospect of capturing the alpenglow and dawn's first light from it, makes a night there well worthwhile. From the hotel terrace you also have a remarkable overview of much of the route you'll be tackling in the coming days.

The first day's trek uses the popular Faulhornweg, long recognised as the finest day's walk in the Bernese Alps, so don't be surprised if you share the trail with lots of other trekkers. It takes you along a ridge overlooking the Brienzersee, cuts across the flank of the Oberberghorn, skirts the base of the Laucherhorn and rises through the limestone trough of the Sägistal on the way to **Berghaus Männdlenen** (formerly known as the Weber Hut), which you'll probably reach in time to enjoy a lunchtime bowl of soup and a drink on the terrace, at 2344m.

You could stay there, of course, but the majority of TJR trekkers either continue to the old *Berghotel* (**Berghotel Faulhorn**) on the summit of the Faulhorn,

300m above Männdlenen, or take a trail across the face of the mountain and descend past the Bachsee – surely one of the most beautiful of all alpine lakes – to spend the night at the **First gondola station**: with its dormitories, first-class facilities, and meals in the restaurant looking out at the Eiger, this is a site of peace and tranquillity when the last gondola has descended to Grindelwald.

The second stage goes to the Grosse Scheidegg, then swings south-westward below the **Wetterhorn**. There is the option of either climbing through a glacier gorge to spend a night at the Swiss Alpine Club's **Gleckstein Hut**, perched on the slopes of the Wetterhorn at 2317m with a fine view of the Schreckhorn, or dropping down towards Grindelwald and

The Mönch and Jungfrau seen from above Mürren (Photo: Jonathan Willia

staying overnight in **Hotel Wetterhorn**, which has modestly priced dormitory options. The hotel is perfectly placed for the next day's optional stage to **Berghaus Bäregg**, located high above the Lower Grindelwald glacier's gorge, with its face

towards the Fiescherwand. If you choose not to visit Berghaus Bäregg, the next stage leads directly to Alpiglen at the foot of the Eiger's *Nordwand* (north face).

The way to **Berghaus Alpiglen** is an exciting one in which you scale glacial

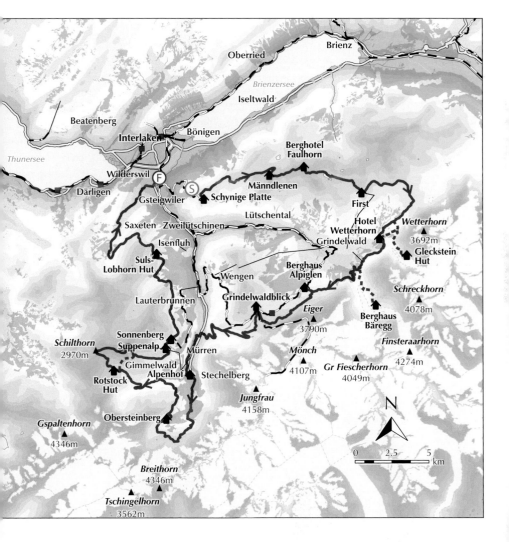

slabs by ladder, and take an airy trail high above Grindelwald. Berghaus Alpiglen

'the main building resonates with mountaineering history associated with early attempts on the Eiger'

has a couple of dormitories in an annexe, while the main building resonates with mountaineering history associated with early attempts on the Eiger. And when you leave, it is by the Eiger Trail that you make your way to Kleine Scheidegg to spend the next night at **Berghaus Grindelwaldblick**. This has dormitory accommodation above the restaurant and a direct view of the Eiger's *Nordwand*.

A steep moraine wall banks the Eiger glacier. Along its crest runs a narrow path, and when the moraine ends the path continues down through woods and pastures to Mettlenalp below Mönch and Jungfrau, then carries on down, down and ever more steeply down to the bed of the Lauterbrunnen Valley more than 1200m below where you began. Then it's

Owned by the Stechelberg Ski Club, the Rotstock Hut has plenty of atmosphere and some fine views

a short, almost level stroll to **Stechelberg** at the valley roadhead, where overnight accommodation can be found in a small hotel or in the atmospheric **Alpenhof**. A one-time *Naturfreundehaus* ('Friends of Nature' house), this is now a private hostel with self-catering facilities, owned and run by a friendly and hospitable couple whose knowledge and enthusiasm for the region is contagious.

The second half of the TJR pushes into the wild inner recesses of the Lauterbrunnen Valley – a landscape of hanging glaciers and waterfalls – in which a night is spent in one of two romantic

The slowly revolving summit restaurant on the Schilthorn provides a splendid panoramic view of the Lauterbrunnen Wall

old Berghotels (the **Obersteinberg** or the Tschingelhorn) seemingly lost to the 21st century. The route then crosses a grassy shoulder before plunging 800m or more into the narrow Sefinental. Having descended all that way, you then have to climb steeply out of the valley to gain the **Rotstock Hut** after a tough 5 hours of trekking.

Owned by the Stechelberg Ski Club, the Rotstock Hut is a conventional mountain refuge, open to all and, once again, with plenty of atmosphere and a fine view of the Jungfrau. When you leave next morning, you could, if conditions allow, make the ascent of the **Schilthorn** (2970m) by way of its west ridge, or you could take a relatively short and easy route to the Blumental above

Mürren. The ascent of the Schilthorn is an entertaining route, with some steep and narrow sections aided by fixed cables and iron stanchions, and with panoramic views taking in all the mountains that make up the so-called Lauterbrunnen Wall – but when you reach the summit you discover a revolving restaurant and a cinema showing sections of a James Bond movie filmed there! The Schilthorn is, of course, accessed by a cableway from Mürren, but the TJR ignores this and descends to the Blumental just above Mürren, where there's a choice of two *pensions* in which to stay (**Suppenalp** and **Sonnenberg**), both of which have dormitory options.

The final stage of the TJR leads round to the **Suls-Lobhorn Hut**, another old favourite, set on the edge of a little meadow sliced with limestone runnels. The hut, cosy and convivial, but with basic outdoor washroom (pray for good weather before using it) and 'standalone' toilets, looks out at Eiger, Mönch and Jungfrau; with the Lauterbrunnen Valley far below, it makes a memorable counterpart to the Schynige Platte *Berghotel* where the first night of the tour was spent.

Next day, a 4–4½-hour trek returns you to Wilderswil near Interlaken, after crossing a 2000m saddle and descending through the gentle Saxetal. Moments before you reach the centre of **Wilderswil** a view opens to the right, and there soars the Jungfrau, as if to wave farewell.

Stubai High Level Route

Location	Stubai Alps, Austria
Duration	9 days
Accommodation	Mountain huts
Start	Neder, near Neustift im Stubaital
Finish	Neustift im Stubaital
Grade	Strenuous
Guidebook	*Trekking in the Stubai Alps* (Cicerone Press)

Austria's Alps are home to a number of excellent hut-to-hut tours. This should come as no surprise to anyone who has walked, trekked or climbed there, for the mountains are uniquely accessible to the outdoor enthusiast without being cluttered with too much unsightly mechanical infrastructure. Yes, there are plenty of ski resorts where cable cars and ski tows lace the hillsides, but walkers and trekkers are spoilt for choice when it comes to relatively pristine mountains. With more than 40,000km of footpaths, and a network of at least 1000 huts to visit, Austria can rightly claim to be the ideal country for the mountain walker. And of the many hut tours available, the Stubai High Level Route (or Stubaier Höhenweg, as it's locally known) is among the very best.

The Stubai Alps are easily accessible from Innsbruck. An hour's bus ride from the city brings you to Neder, a village close to the better-known resort of Neustift im Stubaital. with the knowledge that before the day is over you will not tread tarmac again for another week or so.

The route makes a horseshoe tour of the Stubaital by going from hut to hut over a series of intermediate ridge spurs pushed down from the peaks that almost encircle the valley. A hut has been built in each of the hanging valleys that lie between these ridges, and since some of these are quite close together, it would be possible in certain places to trek a double stage if time were tight. But that would be a shame, for every section of the route is worth tackling without having to rush.

The first day takes you through the Pinnistal, hemmed in by lengthy ridges; that on the left is crowned by **Kirchdachspitze** (2840m), that on the right (west side) by the 3277m **Habicht**. At the head of the valley, the scoop of the Pinnisjoch can be seen, on the far side of which the large **Innsbrucker Hut** (4–4½ hours from Neder) greets the trekker

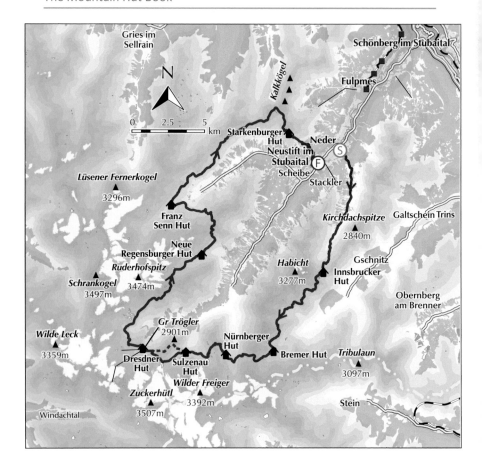

with its promise of a bed for the night, filling meals and an outlook that includes the ragged Tribulaun peaks rising from the hint of a deep shadowed valley. With 30 beds and 100 dormitory places, the Innsbrucker is one of the most popular of the Stubai huts, and is often crowded in settled weather.

On Day 2, there's a lot of broken ground and a considerable amount of height gain and loss to cover, despite staying at high altitude, and with a few exposed sections safeguarded with cables, it may come as a surprise to anyone expecting a straightforward walk. But that is one of the features of this trek – don't take anything for granted. That being said, this is probably the toughest stage of the whole tour, but it takes you among some wonderful scenery and

brings you at the end of the day to the **Bremer Hut**, magnificently located beside a small lake at 2411m.

The next day is shorter and a little easier, with the Nürnberger Hut being the goal. It should only take about 3 hours to get there, but with plenty of diversions and lots of scenic interest to extend that time, it would be easy to fill the day. The crux of the stage is the crossing of the Simmingjöchl, reached with the aid of fixed cables (for those who need reassurance), as is the initial descent on the Nürnberger side. From the foot of screes you enter a basin running with streams, before crossing a glacial torrent and wandering up a rocky slope to reach the **Nürnberger Hut** – a four-storey building of mottled stone, with red-and-white shutters at the windows.

Three hours should also be sufficient for the following stage to the **Sulzenau Hut**. This is one of the most scenic of treks, with the Wilder Freiger rising above its glacier and the beautiful Grünausee providing shimmering reflections. It's the 2627m Niederl that offers a way over the intervening ridge, followed by descent of a steep rock face along cable-protected ledges with the lake in view. If you can tear yourself away from the Grünausee, it would be possible to reach the Sulzenau Hut in time for a tasty lunch and an afternoon lazing on the terrace. Replacing the original building that was destroyed by avalanche in 1975, the modern hut has a long sloping roof on one side that reaches down to ground level, as if to defy further avalanche damage.

'it would be possible to reach the Sulzenau Hut in time for a tasty lunch and an afternoon lazing on the terrace'

From the hut, you can look across the unseen Stubaital to the Kalkkögel peaks, which form a backdrop to the final stage of the tour.

Two options present themselves for the trek between the Sulzenau and Dresdner huts. The lower and easier route goes by way of the 2676m Peiljoch, while the alternative climbs the **Grosser Trögler**, whose 2901m summit is marked (like so many Austrian summits) by a large wooden cross, this one in memory of Peter Hofer, a professional guide who died after a tragic accident on the mountain in 1966. Despite unpromising weather, I chose the latter route for my crossing, half expecting the summit to be free from cloud to give me the wonderful views of the Zuckerhütl for which the Trögler is noted. And what happened? I was in cloud from base to summit and saw nothing more than the rocks a few metres ahead, while friends who chose the Peiljoch option had beams of sunlight and splendid views!

However, you may be glad to have poor visibility at the **Dresdner Hut**, for it sits among the depressing squalor of the ski industry, courtesy of the Stubai Glacier Company; and like me, you may be eager to depart next morning for the full-day trek leading to the **Neue Regensburger Hut**, which nestles in the much more natural environment of the Falbesonertal. Mind you, this is a challenging stage that crosses the highest pass of the whole trek, the Grawagrubennieder at 2888m, and you will no doubt welcome the sight of the hut when it appears at last on the edge of a marshy basin. It's a warm and welcoming place with a homely atmosphere when cold mist swirls outside.

Named after the 19th-century 'glacier priest' who did so much to promote the Ötztal and Stubai regions for mountain tourism, the **Franz Senn Hut** is next on the High Level Route itinerary. The largest and busiest of the Stubai huts, it's often used by the Austrian Alpine Club (Österreichischer Alpenverein, ÖAV) as a base for climbing courses, so don't imagine you'll have it to yourself. The route to

Trekkers with both time and experience may be tempted to climb the lovely Wilder Freiger which dominates the route to the Sulzenau Hut

Looking south from the Stubai towards the Dolon in the distant background (Photo: Jonathan Willic

get there from the Neue Regensburger takes something like 4 hours, with the high point of the 2706m Schrimmennieder marking the halfway point.

The last full day of the tour carries the route along the west flank of the Oberbergtal, a tributary of the main Stubaital. Sloping pastures full of wildflowers and marmots are an abiding memory of this fairly long stage, plus the glorious Kalkkögel peaks, starkly defiant above acres of scree and reminiscent of

the Dolomites. The route leads along the base of the Kalkkögel to reach the final hut, the **Starkenburger**, some 1300m above **Neustift** and with a commanding view of much of the route you've been trekking during the previous week or so. For a last night in the hills, it's as comfortable and friendly a hut as you could wish for. Make the most of it, for next morning your knees will resent the horrendous descent to the valley.

Tour of the Bernina

Location	Bernina Alps, Switzerland and Italy
Duration	9–10 days
Accommodation	Mountain huts and hotels
Start/Finish	Pontresina
Grade	Strenuous
Guidebook	*Tour of the Bernina* (Cicerone Press)

I have a special affection for the Bernina Alps; their snowy crests and tumbling glaciers, their surrounding valleys, flower meadows and hidden places to watch wildlife – these all became familiar to me when I was working there many years ago. In winter, as in summer, I came to know some of the district's very fine huts, and two of my favourites which lie on either side of the massif are linked by trails used on the Tour of the Bernina – a trek that deserves to be better known.

Tempting as it is to think of the Bernina massif as simply having a north–south divide running along the international border, it is in fact an 'island' group with four distinct sides. The western boundary is clearly set out along the Engadine Valley in Switzerland; the eastern limits are determined by Italy's Valtellina. The northern boundary outlined by the Bernina and Poschiavo valleys is linked by the Bernina Pass, while along its southern edge lies the romantic Valmalenco. The Tour of the Bernina touches on all of these except Valtellina, shortcutting a complete anticlockwise circuit of the district by crossing the Pass da Canfinal (Passo del Confinale) or one of its neighbours, and dropping down to Val Poschiavo.

The route is satisfying in almost every respect, and the range of accommodation is such that each night is different.

Pontresina, where the 9–10-day tour begins, is easily reached by train from Zürich. Near neighbour of St Moritz, Pontresina lacks that town's glitz and glamour, which is to its benefit. For this is *the* mountaineering centre of Eastern Switzerland, being well placed for some classic alpine climbs, including the Biancograt on Piz Bernina and major rock routes on Piz Badile in nearby Val Bregaglia.

Directly opposite Pontresina, Val Roseg teases the Tour of the Bernina towards its head, where the Coaz Hut (Chamanna Coaz) can be reached in 4½–5 hours. But a little under 2 hours from

Leaving Pontresina, the Tour of the Bernina travels the length of the glorious Val Roseg

Pontresina stands the **Hotel Rosegg-letscher**, a delightful and historic building at the end of a track used by horse-drawn carriages. With dormitory options, it's a great place to stay – but not at the expense of a night at the Coaz Hut. If you only have the time or cash to stay at one, then choose the **Coaz Hut**, for the route to it and the hut's location on the edge of glaciers make for a truly memorable experience. A more direct route cuts out a visit to the Coaz Hut and climbs from the hotel to join the main route at Fuorcla Surlej.

Having reached an altitude of 2600m, the trail that takes you from Coaz to the Fuorcla Surlej remains high, and all the way to the pass a stunning panoramic view is dominated by the shapely Piz Bernina and Piz Roseg on the far side of Val Roseg. Once through the Fuorcla Surlej saddle, you enter the Engadine Valley region and for much of the way to **Maloja** have the valley's string of sparkling lakes to gaze upon.

The following stage leaves Maloja and its hotels at the head of the Engadine, and strikes through a forested side valley to another charming lake (Lägh da Cavloc). Beyond here, the valley walls close in for the climb to Passo del Muretto at 2562m, where you enter Italy. For centuries, the pass was a major crossing point between Valtellina and Engadine, with goods such as wine and roofing slates being carried out of Italy by mule trains; even today, the initial Italian slopes have old paving slabs in place, suitable for laden pack animals.

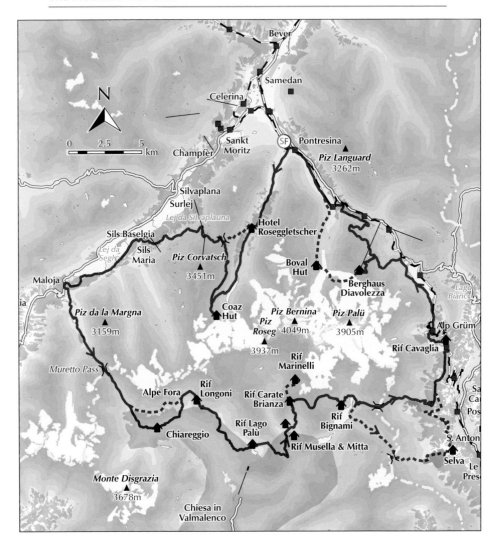

With the stately Monte Disgrazia looming over Valmalenco, a little more than an hour below the pass, a trail breaks to the left to make a high-level route to Rifugio Longoni. The preferred option, however, is to continue down to **Chiareggio**, where the village has a couple of hotels, and next day take a splendid trail to **Alpe Fora** (joining the direct route from below the Muretto Pass) and

continue from there to the red-roofed Rifugio Longoni – another long-time favourite, with Disgrazia once more signalling
its dominance across the valley.

The next hut on the tour overlooks
Lago Palù, and is very different from
Rifugio Longoni. Taking nothing from
Longoni's traditional charm, **Rifugio
Lago Palù** is a light, modern building – a
popular restaurant by day, serving visi-
tors brought by cable car from St Joseph,

*Cascades pour down crags that back the Piana
di Fora on the way to Rifugio Longoni*

and a rather more upmarket hut/hotel
by night. The pine-panelled dining room
looks out at the lake through picture windows, while the next day's trail sneaks
out the back. This onward route tops out
at the minor pass of Bocchel del Torno
and then angles south-east on a ski piste,
before cutting north through a graceful
passageway of trees to a stream draining the Scerscen glacier. Over a bridge
and through marshy meadows it leads to
a couple of *rifugi* (**Musella** and **Mitta**) at
2020m, and climbs on for another 600m
and 1½ hours of effort to reach **Rifugio
Carate Brianza** at the end of Stage 5.

From the hut next day a recommended 1½-hour diversion (plus an hour back)
visits **Rifugio Marinelli Bombardieri**,

'The pine-panelled
dining room looks
out at the lake
through picture
windows'

Looking across to the north face of the Piz Palu from the Berghaus Diavolezza in the Bernina range (Photo: Jonathan Williams)

about 200m above Carate Brianza on a true high mountain trek that provides views of some of the Bernina's highest peaks. Without this diversion, Stage 6 is just a short hike of 2 hours to reach **Rifugio Bignami**, perched on a grassy bluff on the edge of Alpe di Fellaria, with a bird's-eye view onto the milky blue waters of the dammed Lago di Gera. In settled weather, the Bignami Hut is a very relaxing place, with the raw scenery of the Bernina massif looking benign above it. But it must certainly rattle in a storm!

Stage 7 returns the Tour of the Bernina to Switzerland by way of the 2628m Pass da Canfinal, after which you descend towards Val Poschiavo – a valley that is Italian in every respect except for the flags that display a white cross on a red background as proof that you really are in Switzerland. An alternative route descends from Bignami to cross the dam wall at the southern end of Lago di Gera, then makes its way through Valle Poschiavina to make a lower crossing over the border ridge at the 2498m Pass da Cancian. This also leads into the Swiss Val Poschiavo, and both routes eventually merge on the way to the tiny sun-kissed hamlet of Cavaglia, where accommodation can be had at the slightly quirky, family-run **Rifugio Cavaglia**, a thick stone-walled house, typical of the region, with two rooms and a dormitory for guests.

landscape of ice and snow rise Piz Bernina and its attendant peaks. Sheer magic! And this is the view you will have through your dining room window. So what if the route up from the Bernina Pass was not so stimulating? The view from Berghaus Diavolezza will haunt your dreams.

'The view from Berghaus Diavolezza will haunt your dreams.'

The altitude of Cavaglia is a wisp under 1700m. Berghaus Diavolezza, chosen by Gillian Price for the overnight halt on Stage 8 of her *Tour of the Bernina* guide, stands at 2973m, giving a height gain of more than 1200m. This is largely made in two steep sections: the first to a lake on the Bernina Pass via **Alp Grüm**, and the second being the ascent to **Berghaus Diavolezza** itself – a rather uninspiring section through a barren landscape, emerging to an extraordinary scene. Piz Palü with its three white buttresses stands in full view of the massive *Berghaus*, which does a roaring trade with visitors who arrive there by cable car. But it's not just Piz Palü that catches your attention: across a tumbling

This leaves one final day for the stretch leading down to Pontresina. The *Tour of the Bernina* guidebook suggests descending to Val Bernina and following a well-used path that crosses the mouth of Val Morteratsch (lovely views to the Bellavista crest at the head of the valley) and proceeds through larch and pinewoods to **Pontresina station** by the entrance to Val Roseg, where the tour began. But an optional alternative may be possible if guides are available at Diavolezza to escort unequipped parties across the Pers and Morteratsch glaciers to the **Boval Hut** (Chamanna Boval). From here, you then wander down the charming Morteratsch valley to join the standard route to **Pontresina**. This would be a wonderful way to end the tour – but the glacier crossing should not be attempted by trekkers without the equipment or experience to deal with crevasse rescue. Be warned!

Tour of Mont Blanc

Location	Mont Blanc range, France, Italy and Switzerland
Duration	10–12 days
Accommodation	Mountain huts and *gîtes d'étape*
Start/Finish	Les Houches
Grade	Strenuous
Guidebook	*Tour of Mont Blanc* (Cicerone Press)

No summary of Alpine treks would be complete without the Tour of Mont Blanc (TMB). It is, quite simply, a true classic that draws walkers from every corner of the world, a number of whom become so smitten that they return for a second or even a third bite at the cherry. This does tend to put pressure on accommodation though, so if you plan to walk it yourself, you'd be advised to book your lodgings well in advance – then go and enjoy it without pressure.

Every stage is spectacular as you make a complete circuit of the highest massif in Western Europe. On every stage, you trek in view of stiletto-sharp granite aiguilles, massive snow domes or tumbling glaciers – sometimes all three in a single glance. There are at least ten passes to cross (depending on which variations are taken), seven valleys and three countries to visit, and accommodation that ranges from former milking parlours to one of the smartest and most slickly-run of all purpose-built alpine refuges. As on so many treks, it's often where you stay overnight that creates memories as lasting as those made on the actual journey.

Les Houches, the small resort village where by tradition the anticlockwise trek begins, lies a short way downvalley from Chamonix, and has a range of hotel and *gîte* accommodation to choose from. From here, the first pass of the tour is crossed about 2½ hours after setting out. Col de Voza grants views back through the Chamonix valley, flanked by aiguilles, while the summit snows of Mont Blanc can just be spied high above you. It is from Col de Voza that the way to Les Contamines divides. One route drops over the south side of the pass and goes through the hamlet of **Bionnassay**, where a lovely auberge, almost smothered in flowers, makes a tempting early finish to the day, rather than continue to Contamines; the alternative route crosses a second pass (Col de Tricot at 2120m), below which lies **Refuge de Miage** with its direct view of the Dômes de Miage.

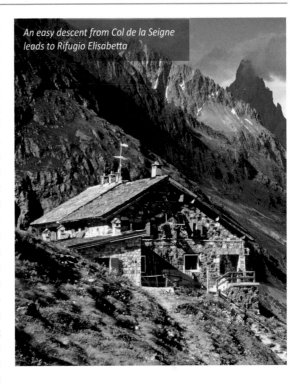

An easy descent from Col de la Seigne leads to Rifugio Elisabetta

Les Contamines is usually taken as the starting point for the second stage, which pushes through the Val Montjoie and, at its head, crosses both Col du Bonhomme and the higher Col de la Croix du Bonhomme, before plunging down past **Refuge de la Croix du Bonhomme** to reach **Les Chapieux** in the bed of the Vallée des Glaciers. This is a tough stage, but there are several options for cutting it short, as well as an alternative ending reached by crossing a third pass (the 2665m Col des Fours), which brings you down to **Refuge des Mottets**, a one-time dairy farm at the head of the Vallée des Glaciers. The Mottets option puts you in a good position from which to tackle the crossing of Col de la Seigne (2516m) next day, a crossing that takes you out of France and into Italy, and from where an exciting heart-in-the-mouth view of Mont Blanc sets the scene for the rest of the day.

As you descend towards Val Veni, which drains down to Courmayeur and Val d'Aosta, **Rifugio Elisabetta** provides an overnight possibility just above the trail, with a close glacier view. There's

'an exciting heart-in-the-mouth view of Mont Blanc sets the scene for the rest of the day'

another hut (**Cabane du Combal**) at the foot of the slope near Lac Combal. The continuing route then suddenly breaks away from its downhill trend and begins a steady ascent of the southern slope to

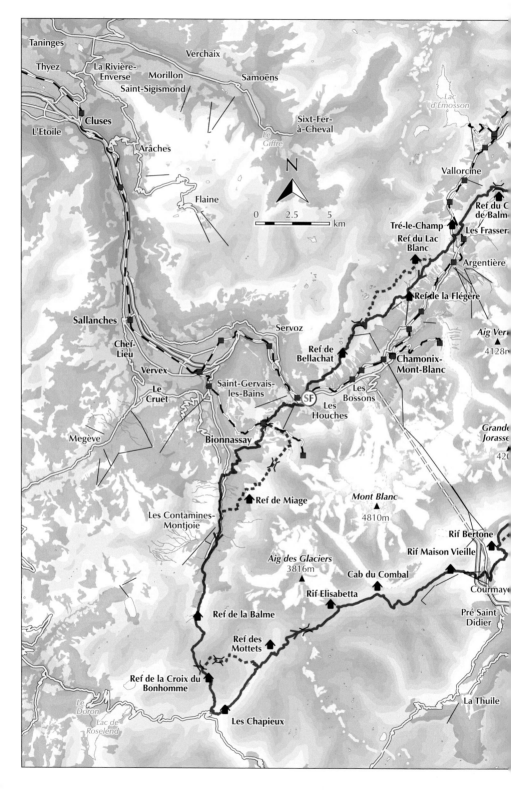

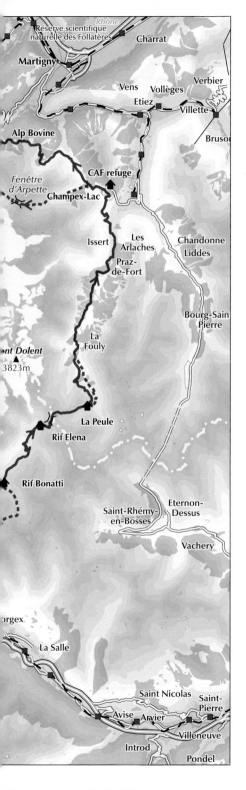

gain a spectacular balcony, from which the Italian side of Mont Blanc and its attendant aiguilles captures and holds your attention all the way to the privately-owned **Rifugio Maison Vieille** on Col Chécrouit. From here, you continue down to the fleshpots of **Courmayeur**.

Between Courmayeur and the Grand Col Ferret, which takes the TMB into Switzerland, three comfortable *rifugi* enable you to choose your own 2-day itinerary. The first of these is **Rifugio Bertone**, which sits at the top of an uncompromisingly steep climb out of Courmayeur. This is just a short stroll from a trail junction offering a choice of routes: one option climbs along the crest of Mont de la Saxe, the other cuts round its flank, and both are so rewarding that you wish it were possible to tackle both. Both routes arrive at **Rifugio Bonatti**, with its direct view of the Grandes Jorasses opposite and Mont Blanc not far off.

The third hut is **Rifugio Elena**, conveniently placed at the head of the valley. It stands close to the start of the climb to the 2537m Grand Col Ferret, with its view back along the length of both Vals Ferret and Veni to the Col de la Seigne, which brought you into Italy 3 days or so ago. The onward trail winds down into the Swiss Val Ferret, a pastoral delight and one of my favourite sections of the whole TMB. Surprisingly, many people either hurry through or dismiss the valley as uninteresting. On the contrary, I find it a sheer delight with its unspoilt villages, lovely meadows and forests all backed

Lac Blanc, with its classic view of Mont Blanc and the Aiguilles

by outliers of the Mont Blanc massif. And there are some charming places to stay overnight too.

The lakeside resort village of **Champex-Lac** (or Champex) is at a crossroads of major trekking routes, for the Walker's Haute Route (from Chamonix to Zermatt) and the TMB come together here for a single night's rest before moving on. Rucksacks and walking boots are de rigueur in once-sophisticated Champex, and on arrival after a day's trek through the Val Ferret, you'll hear much about the merits of the different routes being discussed in the bars, restaurants and *gîtes* that line the single street.

The two routes (TMB and Chamonix to Zermatt) share the same trails between Champex and Trient, although in opposite directions. The main TMB goes via the **Alp Bovine** and Col de la Forclaz,

while a challenging variant crosses the wonderful 2665m **Fenêtre d'Arpette** – the finest and most authentic 'mountain pass' of the whole route. On the approach there's a boulder field to negotiate, and a steep slope of unstable scree and grit leading to the rocky cleft of the Fenêtre, but when you emerge through that gap, you're confronted by a close view of the Trient glacier caught in a motionless cascade of ice, while the continuing trail spirals down to a mere hint of a valley. Exhausting – but a truly rewarding route.

After leaving **Trient**, you return to France at the Col de Balme. Suddenly, a new world opens before you: the Chamonix valley far below flanked on the right by the Aiguilles Rouges and on the left by the Aiguilles Verte and Drus, and the shining dome of Mont Blanc itself. Pure magic

in a single view! There's a refuge on the actual pass (**Refuge du Col de Balme**), but few choose to stay there, preferring to descend via the Aiguillette des Posettes to a *gîte* in either **Tré-le-Champ** or **Les Frasserands**. This puts you in a good position to tackle the steep climb next day to the high scenic trail of the Grand Balcon Sud. It is a steep climb too, much of it on a series of metal ladders bolted to a band of cliffs! If this sounds off-putting and you tend to suffer from vertigo, an alternative path avoids all this by making a more gentle ascent from just below the road pass of Col des Montets. The two routes rejoin at the path junction of Tête aux Vents, marked by a huge cairn.

Once again, you're faced with two options for overnight lodging. The 'standard' TMB stage ends at **Refuge de la Flégère** below a cable car station; the other option is **Refuge du Lac Blanc**, almost 500m above Flégère and set beside the lovely lake from which it takes its name, and from whose shore a spectacular view is to be had across the great depths of the Chamonix valley to Mont Blanc and the Aiguilles.

Many TMB trekkers make the final day a tough one by crossing the 2368m Col du Brévent and descending a knee-punishing 1500m to Les Houches. My preference is to break that descent at **Refuge de Bellachat**, a small timber-built hut with basic facilities, but with a warm welcome from the *gardienne* (warden) and an unforgettable last-night-in-the-mountains view of Mont Blanc and the long tongue of the Bossons glacier directly opposite. Next day, you can face the rest of the descent to **Les Houches** at a leisurely pace.

Tour of Val de Bagnes

Location	Pennine Alps, Valais, Switzerland
Duration	6–7 days
Accommodation	Mountain huts and hotels
Start/Finish	Le Châble
Grade	Strenuous
Guidebook	None, but sections of the route are described in *Walking in the Valais* (Cicerone Press)

With the bold, snowy massif of the Grand Combin (a Mont Blanc lookalike) at its head, the Val de Bagnes holds a lot of appeal for trekkers and mountaineers, while the valley sides are so abrupt that 'ordinary' walking routes are somewhat limited. Bearing this in mind, the little-known week-long tour outlined here is ideal for experienced trekkers, using some challenging but visually spectacular trails in order to visit each of the huts within its boundaries.

As for the Val de Bagnes itself, from its headwall which carries the Swiss–Italian border, the valley drains north and north-west to spill into the Rhône below the vineyards of Martigny. Ski mountaineers traverse the Combin massif on the classic Haute Route from Mont Blanc to the Matterhorn, and trekkers tackling the Walker's Haute Route from Chamonix to Zermatt wander some of the trails on the valley's right flank shared by the Val de Bagnes Tour. There are five splendid huts on the mountains to stay in, hotels in the valley, and cableways at the start that provide an opportunity to vary the itinerary to suit your own needs.

Le Châble, where the tour begins, is reached from Martigny by a branch line of the St Bernard Express – one of Switzerland's slowest 'express' trains. On arrival, you're faced with several options to reach Cabane du Mont-Fort, the first hut of the tour, which stands 1600m above Le Châble at 2457m. There's a steep 6–6½-hour walk using trails adopted by the Chamonix to Zermatt trek, or opportunities to shorten that by taking a cableway or bus to the well-known ski resort of **Verbier**, and then either walking from there (in 3 hours via Clambin) or riding a gondola from Verbier to within an hour's walk of the hut. Whichever option you choose, a night at **Cabane du Mont-Fort** will be worth taking for its outstanding

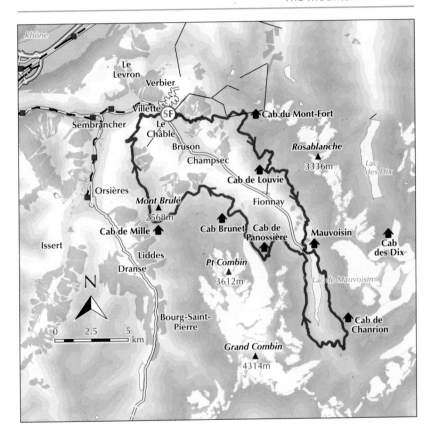

view of the distant Mont Blanc massif. With dormitories containing just two, four or six beds, and a traditional dining/common room whose windows look out at that Mont Blanc view, it's one of my all-time favourite huts.

If you 'cheated' and used mechanical aid to get here, it's possible to ignore Mont-Fort and continue on the first day to Cabane de Louvie, some 3½ hours on. In any case, you'll visit the Louvie Hut after leaving Cabane du Mont-Fort by

following one of the most stimulating of balcony trails, the so-called Sentier des Chamois (path of the chamois). Narrow, and exposed in places, the *sentier* edges the mountainside 1500m or more above the valley bed. Concentration is called for, but this is difficult to maintain because the Grand Combin looms across the valley – a bewitching sight that's hard to take your eyes from. There's a good chance of spotting ibex and chamois too, as the trail goes through a nature reserve.

Cabane de Louvie stands at the far end of the lake from which it is named

On reaching Col Termin, you curve round the mid-height slopes of a cirque, then leave the Chamonix to Zermatt route and slope down into a marshy basin to find the timber-clad **Cabane de Louvie** standing just above Lac de Louvie. It's a cosy hut with a warm welcome from the *gardienne* (warden), and whenever I've stayed there ibex have been seen grazing nearby in the evenings.

The continuing route is seriously exposed at times as it makes an undulating traverse of wild terrain on the slopes of **Rosablanche**. Skirting Lac de Louvie, the way climbs to cross a sharp arête whose southern side plunges for hundreds of metres into a hanging valley. After a brief heart-in-mouth traverse, you then descend into that valley, only to climb out again on the other side. After this it's more straightforward, and you eventually come down to the roadhead at the 250m-high Mauvoisin dam, where there's a hotel (**Hôtel de Mauvoisin**) with dormitory accommodation should you wish to cut the day short. Otherwise it's another 4 hours for the trek to Cabane de Chanrion.

This is a terrific stage, given decent conditions. After crossing the dam to its eastern side, you go through a series of tunnels above the long and narrow reservoir, then zigzag up the hillside to gain pastures bright with flowers and running with streams. After passing the little Lacs de Tsofeiret, with views of the Grand

Combin, cross a col and descend a potentially hazardous section with the aid of fixed chains, then proceed over moraine below the snout of the Brenay glacier to reach **Cabane de Chanrion** (2462m) in a lonely, peaceful setting at the head of Val de Bagnes.

Having completed the eastern flank of the tour, on leaving the Chanrion Hut you cross to the western side and follow a trail northward. Sounds easy, but it's anything but straightforward, for it climbs, descends and climbs again so often that it's difficult to maintain a rhythm. There are several exposed sections too, but the scenery is magnificent, especially when you finally arrive at the Col des Otanes at 2886m to be greeted by a breathtaking panorama dominated by the Grand Combin and a world of snow and ice. Some 200m below the col, **Cabane de Panossière** stands astride the moraine bank of the Corbassière glacier, making this one of the loveliest of hut locations, and the perfect place to relax after a trek of 7 or 8 hours from Chanrion.

Below the glacier, there's an utterly charming region where silver streams gather in a dell backed by ice-smoothed slabs, and beyond this, a hillside of grass, shrubs and low-growing trees. A trail takes you up a spur and down towards a mini-gorge, over a marshy area and up to a narrow road where the privately owned **Cabane Brunet** makes a good place to stop for refreshment. The way continues over varied terrain, with the Dents du

Midi displaying their teeth in the northwest. Meadows full of flowers make a fragrant contrast to the raw scene of ice and snow at last night's hut, then there's a last uphill drag with the flag of **Cabane de Mille** seen above the col after which it's named, beyond which stands this final hut of the trek.

Owned by the Liddes commune, Cabane de Mille nestles on a grassy ridge high above Val d'Entremont at 2476m. The original simple wooden hut was replaced in 2014 and now boasts decent facilities in place of the solitary sentry box toilet of old. The hut's location is splendid, for both the Grand and the Petit Combin can be seen, as can outliers of the Mont Blanc massif, including the Grandes Jorasses and Mont Dolent.

The last stage of our Tour of Val de Bagnes begins with a ridge walk leading to the summit of **Mont Brulé**. The ridge is an easy one with far-reaching views. Trekkers familiar with the Tour of Mont Blanc will be able to recognise sections of that route: on show are the lake at Champex, Fenêtre d'Arpette and even the Alp Bovine route, as well as some of Mont Blanc's attendant summits and the stand-alone cluster of the Dents du Midi. But you lose all that when the trail curves across the east flank of Six Blanc, and soon after begin the descent to **Le Châble** where you can relax with a drink to celebrate the completion of this rewarding, if secret, gem of a trek.

Tour of the Oisans: GR54

Location	Massif des Écrins, Dauphiné Alps, France
Duration	10–12 days
Accommodation	Mountain huts, *gîtes d'étape* and hotels
Start/Finish	Bourg d'Oisans, south-east of Grenoble
Grade	Demanding
Guidebook	*Tour of the Oisans: GR54* (Cicerone Press)

Variously known as the Alps of Haute Dauphiné or the Massif des Écrins, the Oisans region is the second highest mountain group in France and home to one of its finest national parks. Surprisingly little known to mountain enthusiasts from the UK, the Tour of the Oisans explores the ragged outer rim of the district and is one of the most challenging hut-to-hut routes in the Alps. A few stages are relatively straightforward and within the capabilities of most first-time trekkers, but some of the pass crossings are breathtakingly steep and exposed, and potentially hazardous in poor conditions, while the scenery is wildly spectacular almost everywhere.

Linked by bus with Grenoble, the little town of **Bourg d'Oisans** is where the clockwise circular route begins. Within minutes of setting out, GR54 waymarks guide you beside an impressive waterfall (the Cascade de la Sarenne), then steeply up a series of narrow ledges with fixed-cable safeguards, to make the ascent of rock slabs walling the Sarenne's gorge. At the top of these, you wander along a lane, over pastures and through patches of woodland to visit several small hamlets of renovated stone houses. Hours later, and nearly 1300m above Bourg, you come to the Col de Sarenne, where there used to be a privately owned refuge. This was destroyed by fire in December 2016, so you now make a 600m descent of the north side of the col, either ending 1½ hours later at one of the *gîtes d'étape* in the hamlet of **Clavans-le-Bas** or continuing to **Besse-en-Oisans**, one of the most attractive and authentic of Oisans villages, thereby making a tough first day's trek of 8 hours.

The next day is a little easier, and crossing the open country of the Plateau d'Emparis you gain unbroken views of La Meije and Le Râteau across the unseen depths of the valley of the Romanche. La Meije is the most distinctive of all Oisans mountains, and the last of the great

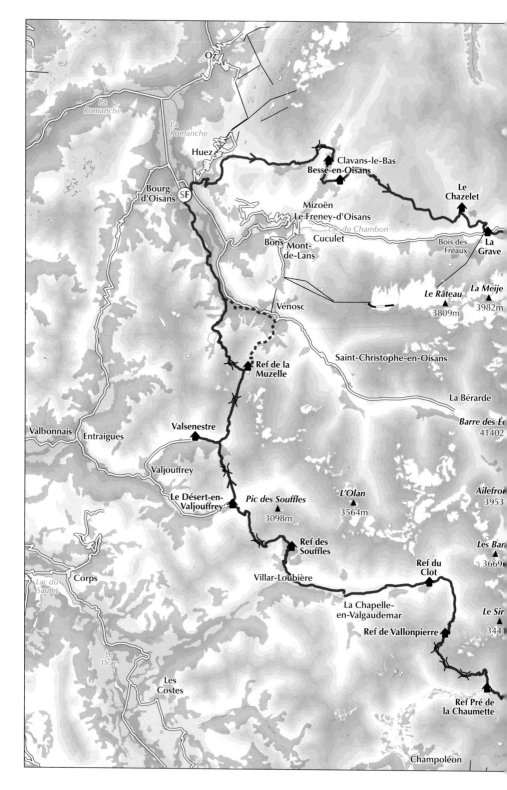

peaks of the Alps to be climbed. Although it is only seen for a comparatively short time, its unmistakable profile makes it very much the symbol of the Tour of the Oisans. Watching La Meije turn to bronze at sunset from either **Le Chazelet** (two gîtes and a hotel) or **La Grave** (three gîtes and six hotels) is one of the unforgettable sights of the trek.

Whether you spent the second night of the tour at Le Chazelet or La Grave, it would be worth stopping at the **Refuge de l'Alpe de Villar d'Arêne** early on the third day. Set among open pastures at 2079m, it's a fine hut with 94 places, and if you arrived there early (it's only 4 hours from La Grave) there's some delightful country to explore nearby, with the Sources de la Romanche being of special interest.

Above the refuge, and not much more than an hour's walk from it, you cross the 2340m Col d'Arsine and descend into an idyllic region of milky pools and streams draining glaciers and snowfields of the Cirque d'Arsine. When you can tear yourself away, the descent continues, steeply at times, eventually leaving the Parc National des Écrins shortly before arriving at **Le Casset** (*gîte* accommodation), less than an hour's walk from the small town of **Monêtier-les-Bains**, where a range of accommodation is available.

The trek from Monêtier to Vallouise is a tiring route which crosses Col de l'Eychauda at 2425m. It's not the ascent to the pass that makes it such a wearisome route, but rather the ski clutter shortly before you reach it, followed by the descent

Seen across the lake from Refuge de Vallonpierre, Le Sirac holds onto the alpenglow

and long valley walk to **Vallouise**. But a view of Mont Pelvoux on the way down lifts the spirits and the Vallon de Chambron is not short of appeal, with its attractive hamlets and small meadows.

Beyond Vallouise, the second half of the tour is much tougher than the first, but there are several fine mountain refuges that add to the interest. Although it's feasible on the first of these stages to reach Refuge du Pré de la Chaumette in the Vallée de Champoléon in a 9-hour trek that crosses two passes, my preference is to break it with a diversion to the simple, no-frills Refuge des Bans, which rewards with its wild outlook and traditional values.

Next day, you descend back to the roadhead at Entre les Aygues, then be-

gin the long ascent to Col de l'Aup Martin and the Pas de la Cavale (both over 2700m), before skittering down a narrow and sometimes exposed trail that spills out close to the stone-faced **Refuge du Pré de la Chaumette**, owned by the Gap section of the French Alpine Club (Fédération Française des Clubs Alpins et de Montagne, FFCAM).

There follows a three-pass day leading to Refuge de Vallonpierre in about 5 hours. But two of those passes are the most challenging of all. The first and last (Cols de la Vallette and Vallonpierre) involve precipitously steep and exposed descents, where a slip could be very serious, while the trail linking the second pass (Col de Gouiran) with that of Vallonpierre angles across extremely awkward slopes

Refuge du Pré de la Chaumette is reached after a tough day's trekking across two high passes

The original Refuge de Vallonpierre stands just a few metres away from the larger hut that replaces it

of shale and grit. Concentration is needed every step of the way. But the **Refuge de Vallonpierre** gives an opportunity to relax in a charming setting beside a small lake at 2271m, just a few paces from the refuge it replaced in 2000. With 35 places in four dormitories, as well as hot showers and a wood-burning stove in the common room, it's a lovely, peaceful lodging.

Another hut will be found nearly 900m and 2 hours below Vallonpierre. With a completely different outlook, **Refuge du Clot** (formerly known as Xavier-Blanc) is a homely valley hut, snug among trees on the north bank of the Séveraisse, and popular with school parties.

The Tour of the Oisans passes through **La Chapelle-en-Valgaudemar**,

and an hour later climbs out of the valley in steep zigzags to reach **Refuge des Souffles** on the way to Col de la Vaurze. Rebuilt in 2006, the Souffles refuge is another FFCAM hut, comfortable and with good facilities, and it gives a head-start next day for the crossing of Col de la Vaurze some 500m above it. The col is an excellent vantage point from which to study this western part of the district. Looking to the north-west, the hamlet of **Le Désert** appears as a huddle of tiny buildings, 1200m below. Limited *gîte* accommodation is available there before you set off on the 5-hour stage to Valsenestre via the 2290m Col de Côte Belle, a straightforward if steep crossing.

Valsenestre is noted for its attractive old stone houses, and for the excellent *gîte* Le Béranger in the heart of the hamlet, from where you set out to cross the last major pass of the route, the 2625m Col de la Muzelle. On this, one of the highest crossings of the tour, the final 200m climb up a very steep slope of black shale and slate is guaranteed to make you breathe a sigh of relief on arrival. On the far side, and 500m below, the last night of the tour is spent in the wooden chalet-like **Refuge de la Muzelle** overlooking a shallow lake, with two onward routes to choose from, both of which will get you back to **Bourg d'Oisans** next day.

Alta Via 2

Location	Dolomites, Italy
Duration	13 days
Accommodation	Mountain huts and small hotels
Start	Bressanone, South Tyrol
Finish	Croce d'Aune above Feltre, Veneto
Grade	Demanding
Guidebook	*Trekking in the Dolomites* (Cicerone Press)

This superb but tough trek crosses the mighty Dolomites from north to south in a memorable 2-week adventure, says Gillian Price, author of the route guidebook. Not a route for novice trekkers, the 160 kilometres cover challenging terrain and climb as high as 2900m. (The more straightforward Alta Via 1 is recommended for first-time visitors to these mountains.)

Crossing an impressive range of alpine landscapes, you will experience dense conifer forests, alpine meadows carpeted with wildflowers, and vast rocky plateaus crowned by soaring campanile-like peaks. Day after day will be spent at medium-to-high altitudes and well away from trafficked valley resorts, although still with good facilities along the way, thanks to the many fine huts (*rifugi*) that provide overnight accommodation and meals. Walkers are led through some of the most spectacular scenery the Dolomites have to offer – the Puez–Odle, the majestic Sella, glaciated Marmolada and Pale di San Martino groups – before concluding in the rugged Vette Feltrine. It's best to calculate 2 weeks to allow for a rest day, not to mention the numerous side trips to panoramic summits along the way.

Alta Via 2 (AV2) certainly wastes no time in getting going. The opening day entails a decisive 1900m ascent, beginning at a modest 561m in the main Adige river valley at the lovely medieval town of **Bressanone**. A handy combination of bus and cable car can be used to take the sting out of the climb, leaving a pleasant ramble to the first hut. **Rifugio Città di Bressanone** stands at 2446m at the top north-west-ern corner of the Dolomites and affords vast views and tempting promises of the magnificent mountain landscapes in store for the days ahead.

Next comes an amble past the soaring **Sass de Putia**, where time should be taken out for the climb to its easy summit. Then it's into the Puez–Odle group with its rock needles and undulating plateau studded with fossils. **Passo**

N

0   4 km
0   2 miles

Brixen - Bressanone (S)

Rif Città di Bressanone

Sass de Putia

Rif Genova

Sass Rigais

Rif Puez

n - Chiusa

St. Ulrich - Ortisei

Passo Gardèna

Rif Pisciadù

Sassolungo

Piz Sella

Rif Boè

Piz Boè

Cap Fassa

Rif Viel dàl Pan

Rif Fredarola

Rif Castiglioni

Marmolada

Cima dell'Uomo

Albergo Miralago

Rienz

map continued
on page 176

Rif Passo Valles

Gardena (with hotels if needed) marks the entry into the exciting realm of the Sella. This fortress-like massif is accessed by way of the awesome scree-filled Val di Setus, from which a linked sequence of terraces leads to the desolate upper plateau where **Rifugio Boè** (2873m) welcomes trekkers. If snow cover and visibility are favourable, the following day a detour should be

The fortress-like Sella massif is traversed on days 4–5 of Alta Via 2 (Photo: Gillian Price)

allowed for **Piz Boè** – at 3152m the loftiest point on the Alta Via; there's even a hut up there, **Capanna Fassa**, where an overnight stay is possible.

Many, many metres down from here at the 2239m Passo Pordoi is the Viel dal Pan, an old smugglers' route which doubles as a perfect belvedere for the

Marmolada (the 'Queen of the Dolomites') and what's left of its rapidly shrinking glacier sheet. The perfectly located **Rifugio Viel dal Pan** helps prolong this lovely stretch, with its prospects for refreshments or lunch; and when you can drag yourself away, the ensuing descent concludes at Lago Fedaia and the cosy **Rifugio Castiglioni** (2050m). AV2 continues easily downhill to the modest ski resort of Malga Ciapela for an optional visit, aided by cable car, to the upper reaches of the **Marmolada** and its thought-provoking legacy of World War I hostilities, with a museum and man-made caverns and trenches.

The trek moves on towards the next landmark group, the Pale di San Martino, for three adventure-packed stages. **Rifugio Passo Valles** marks the start of moderately exposed paths aided with cable and rails, leading into a superb isolated valley lined by the Focobon peaks which dominate **Rifugio Mulaz**.

Passo delle Farangole is followed by a long descent on rungs and ladders – not for the faint-hearted. Afterwards, a beautiful and moderately exposed path continues high above the deep incision of Val delle Comelle, leading up to **Rifugio Rosetta** at 2581m – an oasis in 'the most wild and sterile of deserts' according to mountaineer Leslie Stephen, who visited in 1869; this is the Altopiano delle Pale di San Martino. The spectacular undulating plateau covers over 50km², and is pitted with *buse* or dolinas. Walkers need to follow waymarks carefully here to avoid twisting an ankle, especially with snow cover and mist which can roll in with no warning. If needs be, Rifugio Rosetta is a handy spot for leaving the trek, thanks to a nearby cable car to San Martino di Castrozza, with buses to the railhead at Feltre.

A short but thrilling via ferrata ends at Passo del Ball, named after the pioneering Irish climber John Ball, who became the first president of the Alpine Club. A dip into Val Canali touches on **Rifugio Pradidali** on its rock perch, perfectly located to admire the soaring Sass Maor. This is a handy spot to take a break overnight and draw breath prior to the haul over the breathtaking 2695m Passo

'Rifugio Pradidali on its rock perch, perfectly located to admire the soaring Sass Maor'

delle Lede, where a long stop is warranted to savour the magnificent views. A further roller coaster ends at **Rifugio Passo Cereda** on the road pass, where many trekkers call it a day after ten superb stages.

However, the final three stages of AV2 cross the Alpe Feltrine, a rugged and starkly beautiful range at the southernmost edge of the Dolomites. Drawn-out scrambles and traverses are the name of the day, often in the presence of swirling cloud that is a trademark here due to the vicinity of the plain. In between the two huts (**Rifugio Boz** and **Rifugio dal Piaz**), a good 6 hours apart, a marked sense of isolation is felt, while a final detour via the

Rifugio Rosetta is an oasis in a desert of stone (Photo: Gillian Price)

panoramic Monte Pavione is inviting for walkers not keen on rushing back to civilisation – although the relaxed Renaissance town of Feltre, conveniently reached by bus from **Passo di Croce d'Aune**, makes an attractive conclusion to the AV2.

Tour of the Wilder Kaiser

Location	Kaisergebirge, Northern Limestone Alps, Austria
Duration	3 days
Accommodation	Mountain huts
Start	Eichelwang (suburb of Kufstein)
Finish	Kufstein
Grade	Demanding
Guidebook	None, but see *Walking in Austria* (Cicerone Press) for individual sections

The first point to make about this adventurous 3-day outing is that the middle stage contains some very exciting *Klettersteig* (via ferrata) routes with a high degree of exposure, and therefore cannot be recommended to anyone with a fear of heights. Safety helmets and via ferrata equipment such as harness, slings and karabiners should also be used. The tour itself has no official recognition, but simply links three very fine day walks to create an unforgettable circuit. That being said, it's an exhilarating tour with glorious rock scenery throughout, and both huts we use have views that will remain with you for a long time.

Perhaps not as well known to walkers and climbers from the UK as some other regions of the Eastern Alps, the Kaisergebirge mountains are understandably popular with Austrian and German enthusiasts, for they form a small portion of the range known as the Northern Limestone Alps, which either carries or runs close to Austria's border with Bavaria (Germany). The mountains form two parallel lines – Zahmer Kaiser to the north, Wilder Kaiser to the south – the two being joined by a narrow rib of limestone on which stands the Stripsenjochhaus. The Wilder Kaiser boasts the highest summits and is a rock climber's playground, but it also hosts a number of well-defined paths and lots of privately owned huts and farm restaurants that attract walkers too.

The old town of **Kufstein** lies on the east bank of the River Inn a little south of the Bavarian border, easily reached from the Innsbruck–Munich autobahn, and with the Kaisergebirge looming a short distance to the east, it is the obvious place to start. The trek actually begins in the suburb of **Eichelwang**, and soon climbs a long flight of steps above a ravine to gain entry to the Kaisertal – the valley that divides the Wilder and Zahmer Kaiser mountains. The way then eases among open meadows and mixed woodland on a lovely trek between crowding peaks.

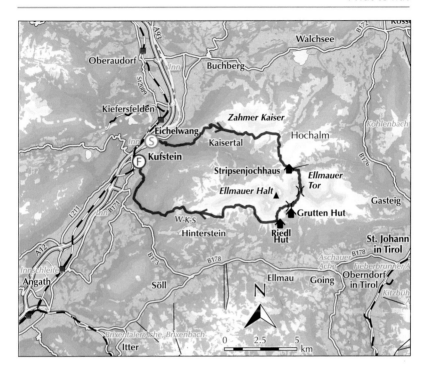

There are several path options, one of which goes to Hinterbärenbad, otherwise known as the Anton-Karg-Haus, in the bed of the valley; but my preference is to take a higher and more open route to the Vorderkaiserfelden Hut, after which a *Höhenweg* (high-level trail) leads across the flanks of the **Zahmer Kaiser**, crossing screes and ducking in and out of woodland before coming to the aptly named **Hochalm** (1403m) on a broad saddle of pastureland, where much-needed drinks are available.

It is here that the trek swings to the south, gaining impressive views of the big rock walls of the Totenkirchl and Ell-

mauer Halt (the highest hereabouts), just as you come to the **Stripsenjochhaus**, a hut standing on a small pass almost within touching distance of those looming walls. Not surprisingly, it is often crowded with climbers in summer, despite having room for 160 in dormitories and smaller bedrooms. If you plan to stay there, make sure you telephone a booking first.

Day 2 is a corker, for it takes one of the most exciting routes an adventurous walker can experience. It begins by descending about 100m on the east side of the pass, before breaking away to make a long slanting rise against the cliffs of the Fleischbank, and on to the numerous fixed

Through the U-shaped pass of Ellmauer Tor, you can see beyond the green Kitzbüheler Alps to the distant snowy Venediger group

The last of the Eggersteig behind them, walkers slog up to the Ellmauer Tor

cable-aided sections of the so-called Egg-ersteig, one of the first 'protected routes' in the Alps, created as long ago as 1903. The exposure is sensational, especially when you turn a corner and look down on the buildings of Griesner Alm several hundred metres below.

The *Klettersteig* teeters into the Steinerne Rinne – the immense 'crease' separating the soaring walls of Fleischbank on the right and Predigstuhl to the left. The sound of rock climbers at work echoes from one side to the other as you now weave a way steeply upwards from one fixed cable to the next, or scramble up stone- and grit-covered ledges. It's an exhilarating route that simply goes up and up and up, until the cables eventually run out and you follow red waymarks

'It's an exhilarating route that simply goes up and up and up'

all the way to the huge U-shaped pass of **Ellmauer Tor** (1997m), through which the green hills of the Kitzbüheler Alps can be seen to the south, with the snow mountains of the Venediger group rising beyond.

On an extremely hot day in the summer of 2007 I found the descent of monstrous screes below the Tor to be excruciating. The sun's heat was trapped in a cauldron of stone, turning it into a

On the final day of the tour, the Wilder-Kaiser-Steig looks down on the Hintersteinersee

furnace, so I was much relieved when I could escape at last and move on to the next *Klettersteig*, the classic Jubilaumssteig with its narrow ledges and shadowed gullies. Long stretches of fixed cable give security as you work a way through a curious landscape of rocky pinnacles, turrets and towers with more exposure to add a frisson of excitement to an already exciting day. At one point you squeeze through a hole in the rock; the route is then aided by metal stanchions and a horizontal ladder, and this is followed by the descent of two near-vertical connecting ladders, then more fixed cables and a third ladder. And so it goes on. But suddenly you run out of fixed cables and

exposure, come onto grass with alpine flowers, butterflies and birds singing, and there ahead stands the **Grutten Hut**, your home for the night.

Adrenalin settles as you sit on the hut terrace, a large glass of ice-cold beer in hand, with a panoramic view that includes distant snow mountains, and have time to reflect on a day to remember. What's more, the comfortable Grutten Hut is the perfect place in which to rest before setting off next morning on what will be a long but much less challenging walk on good trails and tracks all the way back to **Kufstein** on the celebrated Wilder-Kaiser-Steig.

5 Hovels to hotels

*I found our sleeping-den to consist of a low, arched cave,
formed by two or three rocks, one of which, somewhat hollow
on the under side, had fallen curiously upon the others,
so as to make a kind of vaulted roof...There was barely room
for one to enter at a time, and we were obliged to creep backwards
through the aperture. Within...the floor [was strewn] with a thick
covering of short mountain hay, which gave an unexpected look of warmth
and comfort to the place.*

(Alfred Wills, *Wanderings Among the High Alps*)

Bivouacs, boulders and caves

Today the great number, geographical spread, and sheer variety of alpine huts is a tremendous boon to walkers, trekkers, climbers and ski mountaineers for whom they add much to the outdoor experience. But it wasn't always so. Accommodation in the hills, and the facilities we often take for granted, developed from very humble beginnings, for those refuges used by the pioneers of mountaineering were often little more than primitive hovels, and were not much better than the cold night bivouacs endured prior to making the ascent of many a 3000m or 4000m summit. Before huts were provided for climbers, a bed of straw or of pine needles, with the protection of an overhanging rock, would be a luxury accepted with stoicism by the men

(they were almost invariably men) who strode the glaciers and snowfields of the high mountains in clothing no different from that which they wore for a winter walk at home in the lowlands.

They were a hardy lot, those early mountaineers, for despite coming from mostly comfortable middle-class backgrounds, they were prepared to undergo what many might consider unnecessary discomforts, simply to indulge their passion for an illogical pursuit they often disguised as scientific enquiry.

One of those was Horace-Bénédict de Saussure, the Professor of Natural Philosophy at the Geneva Academy, who made the second ascent of Mont Blanc in 1787, and the following year spent almost a fortnight making scientific observations from a tent pitched on the 3359m

Approached by a steep, mostly woodland walk from Lake Bohinj, the Triglav Lakes Hut (Koča pri Triglavskih jezerih) is a handsome, three-storey shingle-walled building in a splendid setting

Col du Géant overlooking Courmayeur. Four years later, in 1792, he decided to repeat the experience elsewhere, this time on the Théodule Pass astride the Swiss–Italian border in the Pennine Alps, where he had a stone shelter erected for him at a similar height to that of the Col du Géant, to be used as a base from which to study the Matterhorn and climb the nearby Breithorn.

Sixty years later, an English mountaineer crossed the Théodule on his way from Zermatt to the Italian village of Valtournenche, and discovered an old man and his wife camped in a small tent beside what was described as a 'rude structure built of loose stones' (the remains of de Sau-

ssure's shelter, perhaps), which the old man planned to build into a four-bedroom hotel. Sadly, the old man's dream failed to reach fruition, for he died at the hands of robbers in one of the Piedmont valleys later that year. However, the Italian Alpine Club (Club Alpino Italiano, CAI) now has an 80-bed hut, the Rifugio del Teodulo (www.rifugioteodulo.com) overlooking the pass at 3317m. It can easily be reached by a short walk from a *téléphérique* (cable car), and its restaurant is a popular haunt of skiers in winter.

While de Saussure and his like were busy studying the Western Alps, Count Franz von Salm-Reifferscheid had his eyes set on the elegant 3798m Grossglockner, the highest mountain in Austria, which soars above the tiny village of Heiligenblut. To aid its ascent, two local carpenter-brothers were commissioned to build a couple of wooden huts on the mountain, from which an attempt could be made. On 27 July 1800, no fewer than 62 people spent the night in the lower

> 'two local carpenters were commissioned to build a couple of wooden huts on the mountain'

hut; and the following day, von Salm accompanied a select group of guides to the upper building where he waited until word came that the Grossglockner's summit had been reached, after which he allowed himself to be carried in triumph down the Leiter glacier on a sledge. Eighty years after the first ascent, the Erzherzog-Johann Hut (www.erzherzog-johann-huette.at) was erected at the Adlersruhe, just 350m below the summit.

But it was that veil of scientific enquiry that was one of the prime reasons (or excuses) used by early mountain explorers to justify their growing passion for wild places. Swiss geologist Louis Agassiz was one of the most determined of these. In the 1840s, he came to study the icefields of the Bernese Alps from

what was at first nothing more than a bivouac under a large overhanging slab of rock perched on the central moraine of the Unteraar glacier. To begin with, this simple *gîte* was partly protected from the weather by a stone wall and a blanket stretched across its entrance. But it was soon extended into a three-room timber and canvas cabin, rather grandly named the Hôtel des Neuchâtelois, in which Agassiz and his companions spent five consecutive summers undertaking experiments and making observations of the glacier itself. And it was from here that, along with Édouard Desor and James David Forbes, he set out to make his ascent of the Jungfrau in 1841.

At best, such a primitive *gîte* would have been draughty, cold and damp, but today's mountaineers, with some of the highest summits of the Bernese Alps as an objective, can spend a rather more comfortable night in the Lauteraar Hut (www.sac-zofingen.ch), owned by the Swiss Alpine Club (Schweizer Alpen-Club, SAC). The hut stands high above Agassiz's historic site at 2393m, with tremendous views to a confluence of glaciers, and the majestic Finsteraarhorn as a backdrop.

Loathsome dens

In the 19th century, before the widespread provision of huts, those who laid the foundations of mountaineering had to come to terms with standards of food and lodging that invariably failed to meet their own. They might expect little or no facilities at all on the mountains, but down in the valleys it was often little better, for once the well-defined way was left behind, travel among the Alps was not only rough and perilous, and the topography confused by unreliable maps, but it almost inevitably involved the use of lodgings that left much to be desired. Conventional inns and hotels were often in scarce supply, and in some valleys the native population lived almost medieval lives, as Alfred Wills later recalled in his *Wanderings Among the High Alps* after spending a night in the home of a parish priest ('the dirtiest specimen of humanity I ever beheld'), which lacked the cleanliness that would have been the norm for this highly respected barrister and future judge.

'We had three rooms opening out of one another,' he said. 'The middle room had a bed, supported on three boards laid on tressels...In each of the side rooms... were a bed, a chair, a table made of an unshaped block of wood on three legs, and a pie-dish. The floors were so thick in dirt, that your boots left foot-marks as you walked across the room; and everything you touched soiled your hands. We could get scarcely anything to eat – a serious evil after eleven hours' walk...and we went to bed hungry and tired. Fleas were seen, and we laid ourselves down in fear and trembling.'

'*Fleas were seen, and we laid ourselves down in fear and trembling.*'

Even as late as 1894, when WM Conway marched almost the length of the Alps, as recorded in *The Alps from End to End*, the old Vanoise village of Tignes (which now lies below the Lac du Chevril reservoir) was graced by the Grand Hôtel des Touristes, in which (according to Conway) cows were installed in the kitchen. 'I doubt whether the Alps hold a fouler inn,' he raged. 'No cheese-maker's chalet that ever I entered compared for filth with this loathsome den.'

As Conway hinted, away from villages it was sometimes possible to find a deserted alpine chalet that could be used for a night's shelter. ES Kennedy and the Rev JF Hardy did just that when they travelled to Pontresina in 1861 with the aim of climbing Piz Bernina. With local brothers Peter and Fleuri Jenni and a third man, referred to only as Alexander, to guide them, they made their way along the Val Morteratsch towards the finest arc of glacier mountains in eastern Switzerland, arriving at a herdsmen's chalet near the site of the present Boval Hut (Chamanna Boval, www.boval.ch). As it was empty, they made themselves at home as best they could. But it was not long before the owners arrived with their animals. As Kennedy later wrote in *Peaks, Passes and Glaciers*: 'The goatherd and the shepherd were followed by the goats and the sheep...These were closely followed by a she-ass and her foal.'

It was not quite what they'd hoped would provide rest before setting out on a major climb, so it is no wonder that in one of his later guidebooks, Baedeker was to warn against using such chalets, for 'Whatever poetry there may be theoretically in a "fragrant bed of hay", the cold night air piercing abundant apertures, the ringing of the cow bells, the grunting of the pigs, and the undiscarded garments, hardly conduce to refreshing slumber.' (*The Eastern Alps*, 1888 edition)

The experience of Kennedy and Hardy below the Bernina was echoed by that of Edward Whymper and AW Moore in 1864 on their way to make the first crossing of the Moming Pass above Zinal. Looking for somewhere to rest for the night, they took advantage of a cheesemaker's hut in the spectacular Arpitetta cirque below the west face of the Weisshorn. Failing to meet expectations, it was depicted by Whymper as a hovel, 'without a door or window; surrounded by quagmires of ordure, and dirt of every description.' Moore described the floor as 'a sea of filth, into which we sank above our ankles.'

In 1953, almost 100 years after that took place, seven Val d'Anniviers guides built a small refuge for climbers in that same Arpitetta cirque to encourage mountaineering in what is without question one of the most beautiful but more remote corners of the Pennine Alps, and in 1995 Cabane d'Arpitettaz (www.arpitettaz.ch) was awarded the Wilderness Prize for its 'exemplary ecological standards, facilities and maintenance.'

Alas, this came a century too late for Whymper and Moore, although changes were in the offing...

Whymper's impression of the Hörnli Hut on the Matterhorn

The age of the mountain hut

The Victorian age gave birth to numerous gentlemen's clubs, and in December 1857 a group of enthusiasts met in London to create the Alpine Club – the world's first club to be dedicated to the newfangled passion for mountaineering. Following their lead, by the turn of the century each of the alpine countries had its own national mountaineering club, with the exception of tiny Liechtenstein, which waited until 1909 before forming its own club as a section of the combined German and Austrian Alpine Club.

The establishment of such organisations shows that in Europe, at least, mountain activity was becoming both widespread and socially acceptable, and in recognising the need for some form of shelter to be provided for the growing number of climbers, the Swiss were quick to respond to that need. In 1863 – the very year in which the SAC was founded – members of the SAC erected their first proper purpose-built mountain hut (the Grünhorn) on the Tödi at a cost of 876 Swiss francs. The age of the mountain hut had arrived. (The SAC now has 152 huts with around 9200 beds in its care.)

In truth, a number of huts had been provided independent of any organisation long before any Alpine Clubs came into existence. In 1779, for example, Englishman Charles Blair gave four guineas towards the construction of a small shelter at Montenvers above Chamonix, which became known as the Temple of Nature and was used mainly as a base

from which to study the Mer de Glace. And in 1787, when the second ascent of Mont Blanc was made, de Saussure slept in a simple stone cabin built for the occasion below the Tête Rousse.

Not surprisingly, Mont Blanc attracted most attention, and to aid its ascent more refuges were built in 1853 (on the Grands Mulets) and 1854, when a small and rather basic refuge was placed on the Aiguille du Goûter at an altitude of 3835m. Some years later, this was described as being 'perched on an extraordinary ledge...the impression of great height and the void opening at the very door...startle all those who are there for the first time.' (Roger Frison-Roche, *Mont Blanc and the Seven Valleys*)

Such refuges as these were built on the initiative of individuals and for a single objective, but it was the creation of Alpine Clubs in the second half of the 19th century that encouraged a welcome spate of hut building right across the alpine range.

The Swiss may have been the first, but they were not alone in building huts in their mountains, for each of the other alpine nations followed suit; and by the time he produced the 1888 edition of his guide to *The Eastern Alps*, Karl Baedeker was able to advise that: 'The numerous Club Huts erected within the last few years...have done much to increase the pleasures and decrease the discomforts of the higher ascents. These huts are generally well fitted up, and contain mattresses or hay-beds, woollen coverlets, a small cooking-stove, cooking utensils, plates, and glasses.' By the end of the century, his guidebooks would caution against sleeping in chalets, unless absolutely necessary, suggesting instead that it would be better to spend the night prior to a mountain-expedition 'either at an inn or at one of the club-huts which the Swiss, German and Italian Alpine Clubs have recently erected for the convenience of travellers.'

BAEDEKER GUIDES THE WAY

Having seen tourists carrying Murray's *Handbook for Travellers* in Koblenz, where he had started his own publishing business in the 1830s, Baedeker decided to produce a series of guidebooks of his own and was soon leading the field, especially with those to alpine countries. His guide to Switzerland, which first appeared in the German language in 1844, ran into 39 revised editions and became his biggest seller.

Born in 1801 in Essen, in what was then the Kingdom of Prussia, Karl Baedeker prefaced his guides with the objective of supplying the traveller 'with all needful information, to point out the most interesting places and the best way of reaching them...'. In alpine regions he advised on everything, from how to deal with the altitude to what to take on a walking tour, where to find the best hotels, the most trustworthy guides and the finest viewpoints; and his guidebooks provided reliable maps and numerous pull-out panoramas naming all the principal features on show.

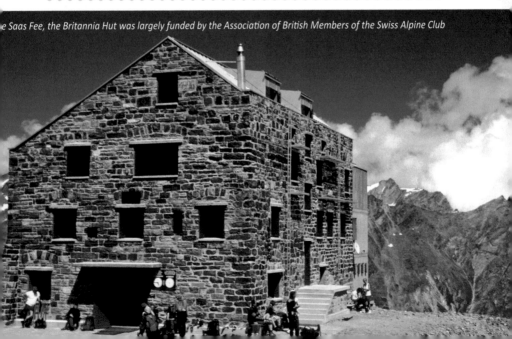

e Saas Fee, the Britannia Hut was largely funded by the Association of British Members of the Swiss Alpine Club

About the time Baedeker gave that advice, Conway, in the closing stages of his epic trek through the Alps during which he crossed 39 passes and climbed 21 peaks, arrived at the Warnsdorfer Hut (www.warnsdorferhuette.at) near Krimml in the Austrian Tyrol. The hut was just three years old, and standing beside the Krimmler glacier at 2336m, it made a great impression on Conway. 'This was the first specimen I saw of the modern elaborate German and Austrian Club-huts. Its like does not exist outside the Tirol...It has a dining room, kitchen and various bedrooms. A clean little woman lives in it all summer and does cooking and service. The traveller can procure a hot meal of fresh meat and the like at any time. He can have a fire in his bedroom! He can buy wine and liqueurs...There are tables and table cloths, beds with sheets, books, clocks, barometer, a post-box, maps, a guitar, looking-glasses, and all conceivable fittings...Such is the modern type of hut, which the rivalry of the Sections of the German and Austrian Alpine Club has generated.'

The amalgamation of the German and Austrian Alpine Clubs in 1874 had not only made possible the construction of bigger huts with better facilities than those found elsewhere, but these Alpine Club huts also took responsibility for the creation of paths and, by the fixing of cables, stanchions and ladders to rock faces, the development of what was to become a rash of *Klettersteig* (via ferrata) routes, which have since spread right across the alpine range and beyond.

Facilities enjoyed by Conway at the Warnsdorfer Hut in 1894 would not seem unusual today. But at the time, unless they had reasonably straightforward access, most Alpine Club huts were considerably more primitive in structure and far less comfortable than this – especially some of those placed in remote and seemingly inaccessible locations.

In 1867, a hut had been built high up on the Italian flank of the Matterhorn at 4114m, followed by a second in 1893 on a spectacular site at the foot of the Great Tower on the Cresta del Leone. Dedicated to the Duke of Abruzzi, it was heated by a small stove whose external chimney faced downwards to avoid being blocked by snow, and had sleeping places for ten on horsehair mattresses.

If not a foolhardy proposition, it may seem at least somewhat ambitious to even consider erecting a building capable of housing several people in exposed places thousands of metres above the valley, but that is exactly what the mountaineering clubs of France, Switzerland, Germany, Austria, Slovenia and Italy were doing. One of these was the Capanna Margherita, built by the Italian Alpine Club in 1893 on Monte Rosa's Signalkuppe at 4554m, making it the highest building in Europe. (The hut was constructed in sections in the valley, and transported first by mules, then on the backs of porters, to be erected on site.)

For this explosion of seemingly eccentric projects we can probably thank

gh above Arolla among the mountains that give it its name, Cabane des Aïguilles Rouges belongs to e Academic Alpine Club of Geneva, but like all Swiss Alpine Club huts, it is open to all

After World War I, the Dolomites were ceded to Italy from Austria. Here, the Sella group is viewed from Passo Cir

Edward Whymper's 1865 ascent of the Matterhorn, for in its wake a surge of interest in the Alps grew beyond the select group of pioneers who had previously treated them as their own. This was to have a profound and lasting impact on mountain communities in practically every alpine district.

The overcrowded Alps

The latter half of the 19th century marked an awakening. Before 1865, many of those peasant hamlets nestling in or at the head of deep valleys would have seen very few visitors from the outside world. But success and tragedy on the Matterhorn triggered a wave of

tion, somewhere as a base from which to explore and admire what they had come to see. What's more, they were prepared to pay for food and lodgings of a higher quality than that to be found in either a poor cheesemaker's hovel or the home of the parish priest. So in common with those villages-turned-resorts such as Chamonix, Zermatt and Grindelwald, which now began to expand, infrastructure was provided to support the needs of these adventurers, not just in the valleys but on the mountains too. As historian Ronald Clark put it: 'Trade followed the climbing rope.'

Of course, not everyone welcomed this influx of visitors. Conway was just one to express his concern. 'The activities of the German and Austrian Alpine Club have no doubt opened the mountains to a number of persons who otherwise would not have visited them, and who profit greatly by the exercise, the fine air, the noble views, that Nature provides for all alike, but in so doing, it has made parts of the country unpleasant to travel in.' But then Conway was a snob, and snobbery among those who were drawn to the Alps had its own pecking order, then as now.

Now that all the highest peaks had been climbed, there was a genuine fear among the early mountaineers that the Alps were 'finished', were becoming overcrowded and destroyed by the very infrastructure that tourism demanded. For those with a desire to climb, walk among or simply admire the Alps from below, the coming of the railways and improvements

interest in the Alps that drew sophisticated, middle-class travellers from London, Paris, Munich, Turin and Vienna. Hung about with ropes and carrying long-handled axes, and led by guides from unheard of districts, they began to seek out some of the remotest of valleys. They needed decent accommoda-

A sublime view of Monte Rosa and a line of frontier peaks and glaciers is to be had from the terrace outside the Hörnli Hut near Zermatt in Switzerland

to mountain roads made it easier to reach what had until now been for the privileged few the 'Playground of Europe'. It was no longer theirs alone, and some who had been there first now nursed resentment towards those who followed. They viewed the advent of tourism as a two-edged sword: it provided better access and more acceptable accommodation, but it also brought the crowds.

Hotels now transformed simple villages into resorts. In remote hamlets or among groups of alpine chalets, rustic mountain inns rose among the meadows in what seemed an idyll of dark timber and stone, the heavy sound of boots and the tapping of alpenstocks echoing along their pine-panelled corridors. In some of the loveliest valleys of Bavaria and Tyrol, rival sections of the German and Austrian Alpine Club financed the construction of sturdy, two- and even three-storey huts, some of whose furnishings compared favourably with that of modest hotels.

Along with the Warnsdorfer Hut praised by Conway, one of the best examples must surely be the imposing Berliner Hut (www.berlinerhuette.at), which stands at 2042m near the head of the Zemmgrund in Austria's Zillertal Alps. Built in 1878–79 by the Berlin section of the German Alpine Club (Deutscher Alpenverein, DAV), today it can sleep almost 180 visitors in its bedrooms and dormitories, boasting exquisite panelling, a chandelier-lit dining hall, and an opulent carved stairway.

And all this, 3 hours' walk from the nearest road.

The Berliner Hut was almost unique in its opulence, for few individual sections of Alpine Clubs in other countries could raise sufficient cash to build on such a scale, even if they wanted to. In 1904, for example, the French Alpine Club (Club Alpin Français, CAF) commissioned a small box-like refuge to be built in the very heart of the Mont Blanc massif beneath the great granite slab of the Couvercle, under whose protective shelter the old Chamonix crystal hunters used to make their bivouac. With room for only 12, in less than ten years the refuge had to be enlarged to accommodate 26. And despite its location being hailed as 'the most wonderful place in the world', it was a far cry from the grandeur of a number of the German and Austrian huts.

So a wide range of accommodation of varying standards spread across the alpine chain to service the needs of an international mountaineering community without greatly improving facilities, and during the inter-war years it was still the norm to sleep on hay-filled mattresses and expect little more than that.

Between the wars

The Alps became a battleground during World War I. This was especially true of the Dolomites, which, a century on, remain scarred by fortifications, including man-made caves to store ammunition and an extensive system of tunnels driven through mountains by men who, prior to 1914, had either earned a living by climbing them or spent their happiest days wandering among them. Coils of barbed wire, rusty from more than 100 winters, still lie curled among the rocks as a permanent memorial to those who lost their lives in the futility of battle.

At the start of the war, the Dolomites had belonged to Austria, but when peace came they were transferred to Italy, and

At first glance, Refuge du Sélé in the Dauphiné Alps gives the appearance of a container waiting for shipment, but once inside it has a much more welcoming presence

many of the peaks and the surviving mountain huts were given new names; thus, for example, the Drei Zinnen became the Tre Cime di Lavaredo, and the Regensburger Hut (built in 1888 by the Regensburg section of the Austrian and German Alpine Club) was given to the Florence section of the CAI in 1920 and renamed Rifugio Firenze.

With the end of hostilities, and with Europe's finest mountains on their doorstep, climbers, walkers and ski mountaineers from France, Germany, Austria and Italy now made the Alps their own. The British lost the pre-eminent position they'd claimed (rightly or wrongly) during the pioneering years of the previous century when they invented mountaineering as a sport, and were now heavily outnumbered as continental climbers pushed new boundaries of what was possible with greater use of artificial aids. Yet the standard of accommodation on offer in the huts between the wars made few advances.

Around Mont Blanc, refuges were still small, comfortless and, on occasion, overcrowded. According to climber and historian Roger Frison-Roche, sometimes between the wars the Couvercle would receive more than 100 climbers looking for a bed. 'They slept everywhere,' he wrote, 'on the tables, under the chairs and on the floor. The wise ones carried their blankets under the broad granite slab which sheltered the hut.'

In 1930, despite having no Alps of their own but a king who was a keen mountaineer, the Belgian Alpine Club built a small hut on the north bank of the Glacier du Tour near the head of the Chamonix valley, naming it the Albert Premier (or 1er) refuge in his honour. They then presented it to the CAF, under whose ownership it rapidly gained popularity (www.refugealbert1er.ffcam.fr). This popularity came not only because it provided a base for climbs on the Aiguilles du Tour, Chardonnet, and Argen-

tière, but also because, being by far the easiest hut to reach of all those in the Mont Blanc range, it received plenty of visits by mountain walkers. Having just 30 places, it would often accommodate twice that number at weekends; comfort then would be in short supply. But it was not until the late 1950s that a larger replacement was provided, and taking account of the popularity of its predecessor, this had space for 140, while the original Albert Premier refuge was demoted to use as the winter room.

The future has arrived

A climber returning to the Alps shortly after the end of World War II would have

About 4 hours from St-Christophe in the Écrins region, Refuge de la Selle projects from a natural rock shelf at 2672m

...ming to be 90% self-sufficient in energy, the new Monte Rosa Hut cost 6.5 million Swiss francs (Photo: Switzerland Travel)

seen very little change in the structure and condition of huts, although some were considerably worse for wear, having been taken over by the military, and a few, such as the Innsbrucker in Austria's Stubai Alps, had been completely destroyed. The Swiss, however, wasted little time in building a new hut, Cabane des Vignettes, in a spectacular position on the Pigne d'Arolla, although when he and his wife stayed there in 1946 – the year it opened – J Hubert Walker complained that it was the coldest he'd ever experienced. 'We rolled ourselves in a dozen blankets each, and still we could not keep out the cold.' The Vignettes is now one of the most popular huts in the region, used by skiers on the classic Haute Route as well as by climbers in summer (www.cabanedesvignettes.ch).

In the brief hiatus that followed the end of hostilities, the number of hut users was down. Recording his visit in 1948, alpine historian Trevor Braham mentioned that he and his guide were the only occupants at the Bordier Hut (www.bordierhuette.ch) for their ascent of the Nadelgrat. They had the Dom to themselves, met no one on their traverse of Castor and Pollux, met just two others on the summit of the Rimpfischhorn, and were part of a 'crowd of six' on the Dufourspitze before moving to the Bernina Alps where Braham spent two nights alone at the Coaz Hut (www.coaz.ch/en).

This state of affairs was destined not to last, and before long mountaineers began to flock back to the Alps, and to their huts. Writing about the Dolomites in 1951, C Douglas Milner told his readers they might expect to find that 'Dormitories with six or eight bunks are available on very cheap terms, and walkers may bring their own food. The same *rifugio* will also provide private bedrooms, often with a comfortable sheet-lined bed... for the man who prefers a higher level of comfort.' He went on to say that 'the cuisine is of high standard, whilst good wines are never lacking.' (*The Dolomites*)

Of course he was referring to huts that had mostly been provided by the German and Austrian Alpine Clubs during that 'golden age' of the late 19th and early 20th centuries, and which had survived two World Wars. Elsewhere in the Alps, the providers of huts were still lagging behind with regard to facilities, and in the years of post-war austerity they were accepted for what they were. But today we live in a different age, and whatever may have been acceptable just a few decades ago has since been overtaken by greater expectations of comfort and environmental concerns.

A steady increase in outdoor activity in the 1960s became a surge in the 70s. The Alps became an achievable destination for thousands of British climbers and walkers; magazines and guidebooks showed the way, and for those who could afford them, a night or two in huts added to the experience. Then came the trekking boom, and hut-to-hut tours grew in popularity, adding to pressure on facilities. With increasing numbers seeking a bed for the night, standards had to rise.

Huts were expanded; they became more elaborate in design and offered more comforts.

Modernisation brought some fanciful designs. In 1983, near the head of the wild Vallon du Sélé in the heart of the Massif des Écrins, for example, the former Refuge du Sélé (a traditional pitched-roof affair) was replaced on a rock barrier

> 'Huts were expanded; they became more elaborate in design and offered more comforts.'

considered safe from avalanche by a hideous but comfortable bunker-like hut by the Briançon section of the CAF (www.refugedusele.ffcam.fr). The landscape to which it provides access is impressively rugged and untamed, but the hut itself must count among the ugliest in the Alps.

Elsewhere in the Écrins, in a tributary of the Vallée du Vénéon north-east of St-Christophe, the Société des Touristes du Dauphiné modernised their Refuge de la Selle with a shining metallic extension that projects over the valley from a rock wall and appears from below like a cross between a snowmobile and a space probe (www.refugedelaselle.fr).

The original stone-walled refuge, built in 1878, could sleep just ten. A second hut dating from 1934 had 16 places, while the latest incarnation can accommodate 75 with a greater degree of comfort than either of its predecessors.

With the new millennium, many of the newest huts, along with those that are being extended and upgraded, are usually now designed with smaller bedrooms in place of large dormitories. Many more are equipped with solar-heated showers, and the days of the 'long drop' toilet projecting over a glacier are drawing to a close as waste-disposal technology used in aircraft (the vacuum-suction principle) is being adapted for use in mountain refuges. One of the latest to adopt this method is the new Refuge du Goûter, one of the busiest in the Mont Blanc massif as it's used for overnight shelter by thousands of summit-bound climbers every year (www.refugedugouter.ffcam.fr).

The first very simple refuge on the Aiguille du Goûter was built there in 1854, and was renovated, enlarged and replaced several times. At 3835m, it was the highest manned hut in France, but with increasing popularity it became an overcrowded and outdated environmental nightmare. But a

Standing near the head of the Lötschental, Switzerland, this is the old Anen Hut before it was destroyed by an avalanche in 2007

few hundred metres away an extraordinary new refuge, designed by Swiss archi-
tect Hervé Dessimoz, was created at a cost
of 6 million euros, with one section jutting
out over a 1500m drop. With the appearance of a four-storey, 16m-high Easter egg,
it's basically a wooden hut clad in stain-
less steel, intended to be self-sufficient
in both water and energy and capable of
withstanding 300kph winds. Solar panels
generate heat and electricity; windows
are triple-glazed, and with good insulation
the rooms should remain cosy in the wild-
est weather. It was opened for business in
2014 and its predecessor removed.

Environmental concerns play a major role in the latest alpine hut designs.
Standing at the foot of Monte Rosa with
its mesmerising view along the Gorner
glacier to the Matterhorn, the new,
ultra-modern, six-storey Monte Rosa
Hut (www.section-monte-rosa.ch) is
said to be the most complex wooden
construction in Switzerland. Built at a
cost of about 6.5 million Swiss francs,
it replaced a more traditional hut that
stood on a nearby site, and opened for
business in 2009, five years before the
new Goûter refuge. Covered by a silver
aluminium shell with an integrated pho-
tovoltaic system, this new hut generates
its own power, and with sustainable features such as a waste-water treatment
plant, it claims to be at least 90% self-
sufficient in energy. The location of this
120-bed hut is truly spectacular, and at
an altitude of 2795m, it can be seen as
a marriage of sustainability and state-of-

the-art technology. The views aren't bad
either.

Not all architects with a commission
to design a new hut strive for harmony,
and some of the latest constructions
are met with considerable opposition.
Perched above the Fréboudze glacier on
the south ridge of the Petites Jorasses
at 2833m, the new Gervasutti bivouac
hut is one of these (www.sucai.it/bivac
cogervasutti). Considered an eyesore by
many when it was erected in 2011, it re-
sembles the fuselage of a plane or a silver
tube with a red-patterned end, projecting from a cliff overlooking the Italian Val
Ferret. But this tube, unlike the majority
of bivouac huts, has modern kitchen facilities, 12 bunk beds, storage racks, solar
power and internet connections.

These are just three examples where
the twin challenges of terrain and climate
have been met by some contemporary
architects with designs that confront
traditional values. The busy Cabane de
Moiry (www.cabane-de-moiry.ch) in
Switzerland's Pennine Alps is another. For
decades this stood alone on a promon-
tory overlooking the Moiry glacier, whose
icefall creates a spectacular backdrop.
Owned by the Montreux section of the
SAC, it is a large grey stone-built hut with
a conventional pitched roof. But in 2009
a modern flat-roofed, glass-fronted extension was added to it. Designed by an
Italian firm, it has a copper facade, and
houses a dining room capable of seating
120, a splendid new kitchen, living quarters for the staff, and four-bedded rooms

for visitors. Yet despite the much improved facilities, its appearance is an affront to the original construction, whose outline matches that of the mountains among which it is set. It would seem that in creating the extension, no attempt was made to blend in with either the landscape or its host building.

In the summer of 2011 I was in the Lötschental, that glorious hidden valley on the north side of the Rhône. With the Bietschhorn at its entrance, the valley is lined with traditional dark, almost black-timbered houses and granaries perched on staddle stones. Beyond the last of its hamlets, I followed an old familiar trail that meanders over bouldery pastures and little meadows, crosses a torrent rushing from a side valley, then mounts an old moraine among clumps

of alpenrose, juniper and dwarf willow. It's a beautiful walk that I'd made several

'It looked as though it had been transported from the old Soviet Union'

times in the past, but suddenly I was confronted by a building I hadn't expected to see. It looked as though it had been transported from the old Soviet Union; an astonishing, alien sight, here among familiar mountains.

This was not the hut I'd anticipated; not the one I'd stayed in a few years before with its stone and timber facade and its

Replacing a refuge of traditional design, the ultra-modern Peter Tscherrig Anen Hut is said to be the most luxurious in the Alps

shallow pitched roof. No, that one, I was to learn, had been destroyed by avalanche in 2007, and been replaced by this privately owned, environmentally friendly Peter Tscherrig Anen Hut (www.anenhuette.ch). Gazing downvalley from its 2358m site below the little Anensee tarn and the fast receding Langgletscher, I remembered the view as pretty much the same. But the hut was something else...Said to be the most exclusive in the Alps, it has its own in-house hydropower plant. It has dormitory places for 32. It has family rooms with

en suite facilities, and two en suite 'honeymoon' rooms with double beds and magical views that catch the alpenglow staining the summit rocks of the Lötschentaler Breithorn. What's more, the hut pampers its guests with hot showers, a sauna, fresh bed linen and fluffy white towels every day. Not surprisingly, it proved to be the most expensive I've ever stayed in.

But is it a hut? Or is it a hotel? It's certainly a far cry from the primitive shelters of long ago. And I guess that's no bad thing.

In addition to the hundreds of huts owned by sections of the Austrian Alpine Club, Austria has privately owned huts like the Dachstein-Südwand on the sunny face of the Dachsteingebirge

Mountain hut timeline

1779: Englishman Charles Blair gave four guineas towards the construction of a small shelter at Montenvers above Chamonix. It became known as the Temple of Nature.

1785: A simple stone cabin was built below the Tête Rousse for use by Horace-Bénédict de Saussure for his failed first attempt to climb Mont Blanc. Two years later he used the hut again when he successfully made the second ascent, accompanied by his manservant and no fewer than 17 local guides and porters.

1800: Count Franz von Salm-Reifferscheid had two huts placed on the slopes of Austria's highest mountain, the Grossglockner, to facilitate its first ascent.

1853: Refuge des Grands Mulets was erected on the north side of Mont Blanc at 3051m; it was enlarged in 1866 to include a kitchen, a dining room and two bedrooms, after which a spate of building saw huts being established on both sides of the massif.

1854: As part of the expansion of hutted accommodation on Mont Blanc, a small and rather basic refuge was built on the Aiguille du Goûter at an altitude of 3835m, making it the highest in France.

1862: The first of the continental Alpine Clubs was founded in Vienna as the Österreichischer Alpenverein (ÖAV). It soon grew to become the largest of its kind, with the greatest number of mountain huts in its care.

1863: Shortly after it was inaugurated, the Swiss Alpine Club (Schweizer Alpen-Club, SAC) erected the Grünhorn Hut on the Tödi at a cost of 876 Swiss francs. It was the first purpose-built Alpine Club hut in the Alps.

1867: Two years after Whymper's ascent of the Matterhorn, Felice Giordano had a hut built on the Italian flank of the mountain at 4114m.

1868: Zermatt hotelier Alexander Seiler paid for the erection of the first basic shelter on the Swiss side of the Matterhorn, at 3260m at the foot of the Hörnli Ridge.

1880: The Erzherzog-Johann Hut was erected at the 3454m Adlersruhe, just 350m below the summit of Austria's loftiest mountain, the Grossglockner, making it the highest hut in the Eastern Alps.

1890: Having spent three days and nights camped on Mont Blanc's summit in 1887, Joseph Vallot had a hut erected below the Bosses Ridge at 4362m.

1893: At 4554m, Europe's highest building, Capanna Margherita, was assembled on Monte Rosa's Signalkuppe by the Italian Alpine Club (Club Alpino Italiano,

CAI), and inaugurated in the presence of the Queen of Italy, Margherita of Savoy, after whom it is named.

, **1896**: The Triglavski dom na Kredarici (Triglav Hut) was erected just 350m below the summit of Triglav in the Julian Alps at 2515m.

1904: With a magnificent view of the north face of the Grandes Jorasses, a small 12-person refuge was built by the French Alpine Club (Club Alpin Français, CAF) beneath the huge slab of granite known as the Couvercle, used as a bivouac by the early alpine pioneers. In the same year, a hut was placed at the foot of the tremendous north face of Triglav near the head of the Vrata valley. It was later destroyed by avalanche and replaced by another hut on a nearby site in 1910.

1914–1918: Mountain warfare affected many regions of the Alps, none more so than the Dolomites, where refuges were taken over by the military, and trenches, tunnels and via ferratas created. Today, remnants of those vertical battlegrounds are part of the cultural landscape. By the end of the war, international boundaries had moved and most of the huts that survived were given new names – as were individual mountains.

1924: Following his successful ascent of the Eiger by the Mittelleggi Ridge in 1921, Japanese climber Yuko Maki financed the construction of a hut to be placed in a spectacular location on the knife-edge ridge itself at 3355m. Costing 10,000 Swiss francs, it could sleep just 16 people, and was given to the Mountain Guides Association of Grindelwald.

1930: The Albert Premier refuge, named in honour of the King of Belgium, was built on the edge of the Glacier du Tour by the Belgian Alpine Club, who then presented it to the CAF.

1939–1945: World War II had its effect on the Alps, all the way from the Julians to the Maritime Alps. Once again, many huts were either used by the military or destroyed.

1960s: A surge in mountain activity brought greater pressure on hut capacity.

1970s: Hut-to-hut tours gained in popularity, leading to a number of alpine huts being enlarged and improved.

1980s: A new generation of huts and hut extensions moved away from traditional designs, especially in France.

2009: The ultra-modern, state-of-the-art Monte Rosa Hut, dubbed 'the rock crystal', costing about 6.5 million Swiss francs and claiming to be 90% self-sufficient in energy, replaced a traditional hut on a spectacular site at the base of the mountain overlooking the Gorner glacier at 2795m.

2014: The old Refuge du Goûter serving climbers on the most popular route to Mont Blanc was replaced by an environmentally sensitive hut with 120 places. **2017**: Capanna Margherita, Europe's highest building, was licensed to house civil marriage ceremonies.

Alpine Clubs and their huts

The first Alpine Club was founded in London in December 1857. The Austrian Alpine Club was next, being set up in Vienna in 1862, followed by the Swiss in 1863. The Italian Club was also inaugurated (as the Club Alpino Torino) in 1863, formerly adopting its current name three years later. Then came the Germans in 1869, and the French in 1874, with the Slovenian Club in 1893. Not to be outdone, the Liechtenstein Alpine Club began as a section of the combined German and Austrian Alpine Club in 1909, but became independent in 1946.

The Alpine Club

Club website www.alpine-club.org.uk Although the London-based Alpine Club was the first to be founded, it has no huts of its own in the Alps.

Austrian Alpine Club (Österreichischer Alpenverein, ÖAV)

Club website www.alpenverein.at *Hut details* www.alpenverein.at/huetten/ finder.php The oldest of the continental Alpine Clubs, the ÖAV has become one of the largest and most active, with 195 branches based within Austria, as well as one in the UK (Sektion Britannia), one in Belgium, another in Holland, and a group in Poland linked with the Vienna section. The UK branch (AAC, www.aacuk.org.uk), which has over 13,000 members, supports the upkeep of the ÖAV's many huts by annual donations to a Hut Fund.

The ÖAV and the German Alpine Club (Deutscher Alpenverein, DAV) are closely linked, and their huts are listed in three different categories at which discounts of varying amounts on overnight charges (not meals) may be claimed by Alpenverein members, including those of the AAC (UK) and those belonging to other Alpine Clubs that enjoy reciprocal rights.

ÖAV and DAV huts fall into three categories:

- Category I: Simple huts or bivouac shelters. Usually located at least an hour's walk from the nearest road or cableway, some may have basic facilities only. Discounted overnight fees of 50–60% may be claimed by members of affiliated Alpine Clubs.
- Category II: Located in popular areas and often accessible by mechanised transport, these huts may be open all year. With better facilities than

Category I huts, members have the benefit of overnight discounts of at least 40%.

- Category III: Largely used by day visitors as a refreshment stop, they may be reached by road or cableway. Overnight fees are discounted by 20% for ÖAV members and members of affiliated Alpine Clubs.

French Alpine Club (Fédération Française des Clubs Alpins et de Montagne, FFCAM; formerly the Club Alpin Français, CAF)

Club website www.ffcam.fr
Hut details www.ffcam.fr, www.refuges.info

Created in 1874 as the Club Alpin Français, with groups dedicated to mountain activities in the various ranges within France, it was given its present name in 2005 as an affiliation of 241 sport-based organisations representing almost 90,000 people. Considering the extent of its mountain regions, and the large number of active French climbers, ski mountaineers, trekkers and hikers, the FFCAM has fewer huts to its name than any of the other national Alpine Clubs, apart from tiny Liechtenstein. There are 142 huts and bivouac shelters maintained by its various affiliated groups. These are not only to be found in the Alps but also in the Pyrenees and the Atlas Mountains of Morocco.

As well as offering a restaurant service, most FFCAM huts provide a room or a corner of a room where visitors can prepare their own food on their own stoves, although privately owned French huts don't usually allow self-catering indoors. Bivouac huts have bunks and blankets but usually no provision of either cooking stoves or cookware.

German Alpine Club (Deutscher Alpenverein, DAV)

Club website www.alpenverein.de
Hut details www.dav-huettensuche.de

Inspired by the Ötztal 'glacier priest' Franz Senn, the German Alpine Club was founded in Munich in 1869 with the principle aim of creating mountain huts (*Hütten*) and developing hiking trails to promote tourism in the Eastern Alps. Within just ten months it had attracted over 1000 members, and four years later it merged with the Austrian Alpine Club

Franz Senn, the so-called 'glacier priest'

(Österreichischer Alpenverein, ÖAV). In 1952 the independence of the DAV was re-established and it became part of the International Union of Alpine Associations (UIAA) in 2013.

Reflecting its original aims, the DAV's main role is the maintenance of more than 300 mountain huts owned by independent regional sections. All but a small minority of these huts are located among the Austrian and Bavarian Alps and, in common with those owned by the ÖAV are listed under three separate categories (see Austrian Alpine Club above). Some of the most elegant of all alpine huts were built and maintained by DAV member clubs.

Italian Alpine Club (Club Alpino Italiano, CAI)

Club website www.cai.it
Hut details www.rifugi-bivacchi.com
Founded in Turin as the Club Alpino Torino in 1863 by Quintino Sella, the Club

Alpino Italiano owns more than 700 huts and bivouacs (*rifugi* and *bivacchi*) across Italy's diverse mountain regions. Varying in size and facilities, most CAI *rifugi* are manned throughout the summer; doubling as café-restaurants for passing walkers and climbers, they can be especially busy at weekends and during the middle two weeks of August – Italy's peak season. Dormitory accommodation is the norm, although two- to four-bedded rooms with 'proper beds' are available in some of the larger and more modern huts. There are no self-catering facilities, and anyone choosing to cook their own food must do so well away from the *rifugio*.

The majority of CAI-owned huts provide access to an out-of-season winter room (*ricovero invernale*), in which a few bunk beds and blankets, a stove and emergency food will be found. Unmanned bivouac huts rarely provide more than a few simple bunks and blankets, so visitors must carry all their own cooking equipment and food.

Liechtenstein Alpine Club
(Liechtensteiner Alpenverein, LAV)

Club website www.alpenverein.li
Hut details www.alpenverein.li

The smallest by far of the European alpine associations, the Liechtenstein Alpine Club began in 1909 as a section of the German and Austrian Alpine Club (Sektion Liechtenstein), but broke away in 1946 to become the independent Liechtensteiner Alpenverein. It now has 2600 members, but only two huts: the Pfälzer and Gafadura. The first of these stands on the saddle of the Bettlerjoch astride the Liechtenstein–Austria border at 2108m; the other is a one-time royal hunting lodge, about 200m below the Sarojasattel. Facilities are similar to those in neighbouring Swiss and Austrian huts.

Alpine Association of Slovenia
(Planinska zveza Slovenije, PZS)

Club website www.en.pzs.si
Hut details www.mountain-huts.net (this site also gives hut details for other Balkan countries: Bosnia and Herzegovina, Bulgaria, Croatia, Greece, Macedonia, Montenegro, and Serbia)

Founded in 1893 as the Slovene Mountaineering Society (Slovensko planinsko

The Pfälzer Hut is one of only two huts owned by the Liechtenstein Alpine Club

Standing below the north face of Slovenia's highest mountain, Triglav, the Aljazev dom is popular with climbers, walkers and day visitors

društvo, SPD) and now the Planinska zveza Slovenije (PZS), the Alpine Association of Slovenia currently has around 54,000 members and 179 huts (164 staffed) and bivouacs in its care, along with almost 10,000km of marked trails. Huts (*dom* or *koča*) are separated into two categories depending on ease of access, with the price of food and accommodation at each hut being determined by its category. There are no self-catering facilities. A few are manned throughout the year, and most have a winter room with open access to basic facilities when the main building is closed. As in other alpine regions, a few bivouac shelters have also been erected. As PZS huts are rarely more than 5 hours apart, some very fine hut-to-hut routes are possible.

PZS huts fall into two categories:

- Category I: Huts located at least an hour's walk from the nearest road. Reflecting the limestone terrain in which they are built, most will have no water available other than rainwater, so washing facilities are limited.

- Category II: More easily accessible than those of Category I, these are mostly valley-based huts. As a general rule, running water will not be a problem, and many will have showers.

Swiss Alpine Club (Schweizer Alpen-Club, SAC; Club Alpin Suisse, CAS; Club Alpino Svizzero, CAS; Club Alpin Svizzer, CAS)

Club website www.sac-cas.ch
Hut details www.sac-cas.ch,
www.schweizer-huetten.ch

With some of the highest and most spectacular mountains in all of Europe, on which the foundations of mountaineering were laid, Switzerland is the quintes-sential alpine country. It was here that the first national Alpine Club hut was built, and where, 150 years later, high-tech, environmentally friendly buildings are replacing some of the older and sim-pler refuges.

Founded in 1863 in Olten, the SAC has around 110,000 members and a UK branch known as the Association of British Members of the Swiss Alpine Club (www.abmsac.org.uk). Through its 111

Tucked against a huge boulder an hour above Alp Sardasca in the Silvretta Alps, the Swiss Alpine Club's tiny Seetal Hut can sleep about 16 in its dormitory

different sections, the SAC currently maintains 152 huts, providing some 9200 beds. A number of other huts have been built in the Swiss Alps by local mountaineering or ski clubs and by private enterprise, the majority of which are open to all-comers.

About two-thirds of all SAC huts (*cabane, chamanna, Hütte, refuge* or *rifugio*) are staffed throughout the year. Most are manned during the summer and winter seasons and on a few select weekends out of the main periods, while each one has a winter room permanently open with basic facilities. While communal dormitories remain the norm, a number of SAC huts have recently been refurbished or rebuilt, and in some of these, family-sized rooms (with two, four or six beds) are available. Showers may be provided in the newer buildings.

While most visitors have meals provided, SAC rules stipulate that if requested and for a small charge, wardens are required to cook food brought by visitors, provided it's simple and can be quickly heated. Personal cooking stoves are not allowed either inside or immediately outside SAC huts, other than at unguarded bivouac shelters. These bivouac huts, often found in remote locations or high on a popular mountain, will have bunks with blankets, and facilities for cooking – some with a supply of gas and working stoves.

217

6 Beyond the Alps – bothies, huts and lodges

There is pleasure in an untenanted hut; in disposing one's gear methodically; in finding employment for hook, table, and bench, perhaps long unused; in starting a fire and creating warmth. The process offers the satisfaction of moving into a new house, but is accomplished in an hour.

(Robin Fedden, *The Enchanted Mountains*)

The alpine hut system has been repli-cated in numerous mountain regions throughout the world, yet in the UK – birthplace of mountaineering as a sport – there is no chain of refuges such as exists in the Alps. There are, however, somewhere in the region of 70 individ-ual huts, most of which are situated in prime climbing locations; some of them are owned by the British Mountaineering Council (BMC) or by one of the larger walking or climbing clubs, but they hardly constitute a connecting chain. Hut to hut is not really appropriate here. Instead, hutted accommodation is used primarily as a base from which to set out on walks and climbs in the immediate locality.

The first UK hut was acquired in 1912 by the Rucksack Club of Manches-ter, when they took over a cottage in the Carneddau range in North Wales. Facilities must have been severely lim-ited, for according to the Club's website (www.rucksackclub.org), one of the hut rules stated that 'sanitary arrangements should be executed in the rocks not less than 100 yards from the rear of the hut.' It closed just eight years later, but the Club has since opened others in Snow-donia, the Lake District and Scotland. Formed in 1902, the Rucksack Club is one of Britain's foremost mountaineer-ing clubs, with a regular programme of meets at home and abroad.

In 1925, the Climbers' Club (www.climbers-club.co.uk) acquired its first hut in Snowdonia. Helyg can now sleep 13 people and has hot showers, a fully equipped kitchen and (most important for anyone climbing in North Wales) a drying room. Also in Snowdonia, in 1932 the women-only Pinnacle Club (www.pin-nacleclub.co.uk) opened the Emily Kelly Hut, a former power station storehouse at the foot of Snowdon. Larger than the Helyg, it can sleep 22 on alpine-style bunks. While this is the only hut owned by the Pinnacle Club, the Climbers' Club manages eight in all, one of its most popular being the Count House, close to the famous granite sea cliff of Bosigran, in Cornwall.

Other notable UK huts include the BMC's Don Whillans Hut in the Peak District. As uniquely eccentric as the climber in whose memory it is named, it is tucked below a line of crags at the Roaches and consists of an atmospheric stone-built cottage and a cave which houses the kitchen. In Patterdale in the Lake District, the George Starkey Hut is owned and managed by the Association of British Members of the Swiss Alpine Club (ABMSAC, www.abmsac.org.uk) in conjunction with the Alpine Club (www.alpine-club.org.uk). With room for 28, it has showers, a drying room and fully equipped kitchen.

Among those in Scotland there's the Alex MacIntyre Memorial Hut at Onich near Glen Coe, and the Glen Brittle Memorial Hut near the foot of the Cuillins on the Isle of Skye, which has accommodation for 20 and is open to members of all clubs affiliated to the BMC and Mountaineering Council for Scotland (www.mountaineering.scot). The Scottish Mountaineering Club (SMC, www.smc.org.uk) manages five huts in all, the oldest being the Charles Inglis Clark Memorial Hut, erected on the north side of Ben Nevis in the late 1920s, with 24 places, a drying room and composting toilets.

Then there are the bothies, those mostly stone-built cottages (often former shepherds' huts), left unlocked for the use of anyone in need of shelter in the hills. In some respects they may be compared to bivvy huts in the Alps, for they have very few amenities – neither gas nor electricity, no running water and only rarely will there be any beds or toilets. Basic they may be, but regular users are passionate about this unique free-to-use facility and arrange working parties to maintain and renovate them. The Mountain Bothies Association (MBA) cares for about 100 of these shelters, most of which are to be found in wild parts of Scotland, with the rest scattered in rural parts of Wales and the north of England.

For a list of all huts in the UK, contact the BMC (www.thebmc.co.uk). For information on mountain bothies, contact the MBA (www.mountainbothies.org.uk).

Outside the UK, huts of one kind or another are to be found in many of the world's great mountain ranges, as the following examples show.

Andes

Although the Andes is the world's longest mountain chain, with a number of world-class trekking routes and mountaineering challenges, there are very few mountain huts. Camping is the answer for overnight accommodation almost everywhere in the valleys and on the mountains themselves. There are reported to be refuges at the base camps of Huascaran and one or two other mountains in Peru, and a handful in Bolivia's Cordillera Real. In Patagonia, however, a number of huts (some staffed, others simple unmanned shelters) have been established in the national parks: in Chile's controversial new Parque Patagonia–Jeinimeni National Reserve, for example, and in the Nahuel Huapi park where a network of huts has been set up by the Club Andino Bariloche (www.clubandino.org), making it possible to experience a hut-to-hut tour in beautiful surroundings. And close to the town of El Bolsón, a circular tour using 13 huts has a growing reputation for tough trekking with atmospheric accommodation (www.trekelbolson.com). In the world-famous Torres del Paine National Park (https://torresdelpaine.com), eight *refugios* provide dormitory accommodation and restaurant facilities for trekkers drawn to its iconic mountains, its lakes, glaciers, rivers, and its plant and animal life.

Appalachians

Established in 1876, the Appalachian Mountain Club (AMC, www.outdoors.org) is the oldest conservation group in the United States. Its members pioneered the country's mountain hut system after building the first of its eight shelters in the White Mountains of New Hampshire in 1888. Modelled on refuges in the European Alps, the staffed huts can accommodate 35–90 hikers, with meals being provided at most of them. All eight of the AMC's huts are spaced along what many consider to be the most beautiful section of the famous ultra-long Appalachian Trail (where it crosses the Presidential Range), thereby making a very fine linear hut-to-hut tour.

Elsewhere in the US, the American Alpine Club (www.americanalpineclub.org) manages a 'climbers' ranch' in the Grand Tetons, and the small but magnificently sited Snowbird Hut (free to use and open to everyone) in the Talkeetna mountains of Alaska, while the Sierra Club (www.sierraclub.org) manages a small number of huts and lodges in California's Sierra Nevada range – there's also an emergency shelter on the summit of Mount Whitney. But the largest number of backcountry huts in the whole of the US will be found in Colorado, where more than 160 huts and yurts (staffed and unmanned) serve the outdoor community; an organisation known as the 10th Mountain Division Hut Association (www.huts.org) manages 34 of these. The Rocky Mountains of Colorado have arguably some of America's finest hiking, skiing and snowshoeing opportunities, and the hut system there makes the wilderness accessible in winter as well as summer. Most of the huts (cabins) have equipped kitchens and wood-burning stoves. A few even boast saunas.

Atlas Mountains

French climbers were particularly active among the highest of Morocco's mountains during the 1920s and 30s, and a few French Alpine Club refuges have since been established among the High

Atlas chain south of Marrakech. With the 4167m summit of Djebel Toubkal being the loftiest in North Africa, the refuge built by the French in 1938 to facilitate its ascent is by far and away the busiest. Previously known as Refuge Neltner, now the Refuge du Toubkal (www.refugedutoubkal.com), it is located high in the Mizane Valley at 3207m. Once, when I was there, the then guardian had the disconcerting habit of standing on his head on the table when my group were trying to eat! A new hut, Les Mouflons du Toubkal (www.refugetoubkal.com), has been built nearby, while in many Berber villages in the mountains, a room or two will be available in one of the houses for trekkers to stay in. These *gîtes* vary greatly in facilities and standards of hygiene, but provide an alternative to camping when making a short tour.

Canadian Rockies

Founded in 1906, the Alpine Club of Canada (ACC, www.alpineclubofcanada. ca) claims to have the largest network of backcountry huts in North America, ranging from cosy lodges set in alpine meadows to remote climbers' huts in spectacular locations. There's the well-equipped Bow Hut at 2350m on the eastern side of the Wapta Icefield in Banff National Park, and the extremely popular Elizabeth Parker Hut (named after one of the ACC founders), nestling among the meadows close to the shore of Lake O'Hara in Yoho

National Park. The hut, which has just 24 places in summer and 20 in winter, is so popular that, in summer, reservations are made through an online lottery! Meanwhile, the stone-walled Abbot Pass Hut sits astride the Continental Divide at 2926m, about 4–5 hours from Lake O'Hara, and is the second highest permanent structure in the whole of Canada. Climbs on the south-east ridge of Mount Victoria and the west face of Mount Lefroy begin at the front door.

Reservations are obligatory for all ACC huts; membership is not a requirement for their use, but ACC members receive discounted rates on overnight fees.

Caucasus

Shared between Russia and Georgia, and acting as Europe's southern bastion, the Caucasus is a magnificent range whose most formidable peaks rise out of glacial basins. Among the most impressive of these, it's impossible to ignore the following three: Ushba, a double-headed Caucasus Matterhorn; Dykh-Tau, whose south face could be taken for the Grandes Jorasses; and Shkelda, a real saw-tooth ridged peak. But to the north-west of these, and overlooking the head of the Baksan Valley, stands the highest of them all, the 5642m extinct volcano of Mount Elbrus, notable for being the highest mountain in Europe.

There are few mountain huts in the Caucasus. An exception was the staffed Priut refuge (officially known as Priut 11), which stood for almost 60 years

on the lower snow slopes of Elbrus at 4157m. Aptly described by mountain guide and writer Victor Saunders as a 'three storey silver sausage perched on a mound of lava frozen in mid-flow', it had basic accommodation for about 100 in small dormitories or four-bedded rooms, and despite being sited almost 1500m below the summit, was used as a base for climbers. (Elbrus is not a technically difficult climb, but the ascent is physically challenging for anyone not adequately acclimatised to the altitude.) Dating from 1939, the Priut refuge replaced an earlier hut erected in 1929 by 11 scientists (hence the name Priut 11, meaning 'Refuge of the 11'). Sadly, the Mark 2 version burned down in the summer of 1998, with the loss of several lives.

A timber-built hut now stands close to the site of the old one. With places for just 20, it's known as the Diesel Hut, while a group of a dozen steel cylinders (christened the Barrel Huts) have been adapted to sleep six in each one. But as I discovered in 1990, environmental awareness is not a strong point here, for piles of rubbish lie dumped nearby, and the toilets have gained a reputation for being among the world's worst. But the mountains are spectacular.

Corsica

Corsica has been likened to a mountain rising from the sea; Napoleon Bonaparte (the island's best-known son) claimed he could smell the fragrance of his homeland long before he could see it when approaching by ship, for the aromatic maquis that covers the hillsides makes its soubriquet 'the scented isle' a very apt one. The fourth largest of the Mediterranean islands, Corsica is truly mountainous, with a long spine of granite peaks and ridges stretching most of its length. The highest of its summits is the 2706m Monte Cinto, overlooking Haut Asco, but it has a large number of craggy, fine-looking peaks whose sun-warmed crags have an undeniable appeal to climbers in search of sport in an off-beat relaxed environment. The island is perhaps better known to the outdoor community today for being home to the GR20 – the classic high-level route reckoned to be one of the toughest treks in Europe.

By tradition, climbers on Corsica either camp or sleep in shepherds' huts (*bergeries*), while trekkers on the GR20 now have sufficient refuges to be able to sleep under a roof for most if not all of the way – but as they can be extremely busy in the main trekking season, and places are given on a first-come-first-served basis, carrying a tent or bivvy bag makes sense. The majority of refuges on the GR20 were established by the Parc Naturel Régional de Corse (PNRC, www.pnr.corsica), but a few are privately owned. All have basic bunk-bed accommodation, as well as kitchens for self-catering, and cold-water showers in the majority. (Solar heated water is available in a few.) They are staffed in summer by *gardiens* (wardens), some of whom may provide meals, while others sell a few provisions for self-catering. The refuges remain unlocked out of season (between October and May) when they're untenanted. Although wild camping is strictly forbidden along the route and throughout the PNRC, tents are allowed in marked *aires de bivouac* next to refuges, for which a charge is made by the hut warden. But beware the scavenging feral pigs that are the curse of campers on Corsica!

A few other huts will be found elsewhere on this mountainous island, while many villages have *gîtes d'étape* in which to stay.

Himalaya

There are no mountain huts, as we know them in Europe, in the Himalaya, but the provision of simple overnight accommodation for travellers has long been part of the culture of the mountain peoples who live there. In Ladakh, 'homestay' accommodation in a number of villages is increasingly used by visiting trekkers. It usually consists of a room (with or without bedding) made available in a local house, with meals provided for those who want them. Amenities will be limited and quite primitive, but the opportunity to witness the everyday home life of the hospitable Ladakhi people more than compensates for any lack of facilities.

Nepal saw the birth of Himalayan trekking in the 1960s, and although the first commercial treks used tents, inde-

An ever-cheerful hostess in a Ladakhi homestay

pendent travellers were offered a bed in the homes of villagers. These ad hoc arrangements developed into 'teahouses' – the first of the very simple lodges that now line many a popular trekking route. The first generation of these were very basic indeed, with no toilets, and opportunities to wash limited to the village standpipe – if there was one. But meals were always available, even if it meant *dahl bhaat* (rice and dahl) twice a day and every day for the duration of the trek. Nowadays, purpose-built lodges with twin-bedded rooms, hot showers, Wi-Fi access and a wide range of menu items are the norm along the trails of every major trekking route, with standards improving year by year – especially on

the most popular treks such as those in the Everest and Annapurna regions.

In Sikkim and on the Singalila Ridge of West Bengal, which extends into Sikkim, a chain of simple – mostly unmanned – 'bungalows' or trekkers' huts exists on trekking routes that edge along the border with Nepal, making it possible to undertake short treks there without the need to carry a tent. One of these is located near the Dzongri meadow below Kangchenjunga, visited in the 1930s by mountaineer Frank Smythe. So impressed was he by the location, he proposed that 'a proper shelter hut [be built there] run on the same lines as a Swiss Alpine Club hut.' Eighty years on, the idea has still not come to fruition.

Picos de Europa

Just 15km from the Costa Verde on Spain's Atlantic coast, the Picos de Europa are like a breakaway group detached from the Cordillera Cantabrica, which runs like a spine from close to the Pyrenean foothills as far west as the Portuguese border. The Picos are a small but rugged cluster of mountains measuring 40km by 20km, consisting of three massifs separated by deep gorges, and protected as a national park (the Parque Nacional de los Picos de Europa, www.picoseuropa.net) since 1918. These mountains are not as high as the neighbouring Pyrenees, for they only reach a maximum altitude of 2648m on Torre Cerredo in the Central Massif, but height is not everything; rising dramatically out of pastureland, they impress with awe-inspiring peaks such as Naranjo de Bulnes, the best known, which is also found in the Central Massif.

A modest number of *refugios*, most of which are manned in summer, are dotted around the various massifs. Not surprisingly, the largest is the Vega de Urriello hut, which serves Naranjo de Bulnes. With 96 places (12 in the winter room), food and drinks are available, and there's a spring of clear water nearby. In all, the Central Massif has four huts and a former *refugio* elevated to hotel status (Hotel Áliva) but with modest prices. The cost of staying in the *refugios* can be reduced for members of a recognised Alpine Club, so take your membership card with you to claim a discount.

While September is reckoned to be the best time to go there, August is the busiest month, and reservations will probably be necessary for some of the huts (see www.thepicosdeeuropa.com), but simple shepherds' bothies scattered throughout the mountains provide very basic alternative overnight lodging. Facilities may be negligible, so expect little more than four walls and a roof, and carry a stove, bedding and food with you.

Pyrenees

Europe's second major mountain range west of the Caucasus has a number of huts of varying standards – both staffed

Standing below the Brèche de Roland in the Cirque de Gavarnie, this is one of the busiest of all Pyrenean huts

and unmanned – on either side of the French–Spanish border. Most of those on the French side are owned either by the French Alpine Club (Fédération Française des Clubs Alpins et de Montagne, FFCAM, www.ffcam.fr) or by the Parc National des Pyrénées (PNP, www.pyrenees-parcnational.fr), while Spanish huts (refugios/refugis) usually belong to one of the main mountaineering clubs of Aragon or Catalonia. Huts that are staffed during the summer months provide meals, while facilities in the unstaffed refuges are meagre at best – often little more than four walls and a roof. A few purpose-built bivvy huts of particular use to climbers can be found in high and remote locations, and some of these are equipped with bedding. In the tiny, mountain-locked Principality of Andorra, walkers and climbers in some of the most remote valleys are served by no fewer than 25 unmanned, free-to-use huts (see www.visitandorra.com) and one staffed hut, Refugi de Coma Pedrosa (www.comapedrosa.ad).

Until fairly recently, the standard of hutted accommodation in the Pyrenees lagged some way behind that of the Alps, but with a great rise in activity on both sides of the range, steady improvements are being made without loss of the huts' traditional uniqueness.

Hut-to-hut trekking is growing in popularity throughout the range, especially in the Aigüestortes National Park in Spain, where a number of manned huts occupy idyllic lakeside locations. Meanwhile, on the edge of the high mountains and throughout the French foothills, countless gîtes d'étape provide alternative accommodation of special interest to trekkers following the lengthy GR10 from the Atlantic to the Mediterranean.

Southern Alps

The Southern Alps represent only one portion of New Zealand's great outdoors. Spread throughout the length of both North and South Islands, there's tremendous coastal scenery as well as fjords, huge waterfalls, volcanoes, geysers and hot springs, and an exotic range of plant and animal species. There's plenty of wild country, with dense vegetation, tumultuous rivers and (in South Island especially) rainfall of tropical proportions. Mountaineering is challenging, but very popular – the New Zealand Alpine Club (NZAC, https://alpineclub.org.nz) is one of the world's oldest, having been founded in 1891. Three years later, the country's highest peak, the impressive snow- and ice-caked Mount Cook, was climbed by a trio of local men. Considering the terrain and conditions experienced in the Southern Alps, it's no surprise that NZ climbers have gained a reputation for toughness. But on top of some great climbing to be had on heavily glaciated peaks, there are many fine treks that enable the country to be explored from hut to hut, the Milford and Routeburn Tracks being among the best known.

A wide variety of huts serve both climbers and trekkers (known in New

Zealand as trampers), with the Department of Conservation (DoC, www.doc.govt.nz) managing more than 900 (the NZAC owns 17). The majority are unmanned, and anyone using them needs to be self-sufficient with all cooking gear as well as food. In the backcountry, huts are similar to the bothies of Scotland; they are usually spaced a day's walk apart and are maintained by local tramping clubs. By comparison with huts in the European Alps, many are pretty basic, with little more than communal bunks and a 'long drop' toilet. Others, such as those on the most heavily trekked routes, have electricity and flush toilets, while several huts built in the national parks have fully equipped kitchens and a warden in charge. Fees vary depending on the class of hut, and are payable to either the DoC or the NZAC.

Tatras

Unevenly divided between Poland and Slovakia, the Tatras are part of the great horseshoe chain of the Carpathians and protected as a national park on both sides of the border. Although only a relatively small group, the granite peaks of the High Tatra, south-east of the little resort town of Zakopane in Poland, contain some challenging climbs and entertaining walks. The climber and poet Wilfrid Noyce once described them as the Alps in miniature.

Huts (known as *chata*) are found in practically every Slovakian valley, while on the Polish flank, where a mountain refuge is known as a *schronisko*, there are eight (see www.discoverzakopane.com). Most are large un-hut-like buildings – the 84-bed Mountain Hotel Kalatówki, for example, even has en suite bathrooms – but the smaller refuges are similar to some of the older and more traditional Austrian huts. All are staffed during the summer, and with good walking country close by. A greater and more varied choice of walks is to be had on the Slovakian side, and a few hut-to-hut treks of between a week and 10 days can be made there (see www.travelslovakia.sk).

APPENDIX A
Useful contacts

Alpine Clubs and UK-based mountaineering organisations
The Alpine Club
55 Charlotte Road
London
EC2A 3QF
www.alpine-club.org.uk

Association of British Members of the Swiss Alpine Club (ABMSAC)
www.abmsac.org.uk

Austrian Alpine Club (Österreichischer Alpenverein, ÖAV)
Olympiastr. 37
6020 Innsbruck
Austria
www.alpenverein.at

Austrian Alpine Club (UK Branch)
Unit 43, Glenmore Business Park
Blackhill Road
Holton Heath
Poole
BH16 6NL
www.aacuk.org.uk

British Mountaineering Council (BMC)
177–179 Burton Road
West Didsbury
Manchester
M20 2BB
www.thebmc.co.uk

French Alpine Club (Fédération Française des Clubs Alpins et de Montagne, FFCAM; formerly Club Alpin Français, CAF)
24 avenue Laumière
75019 Paris
www.ffcam.fr

German Alpine Club (Deutscher Alpenverein, DAV)
Von-Kahr-Str. 2–4
80997 Munich
www.alpenverein.de

Italian Alpine Club (Club Alpino Italiano, CAI)
Via E. Petrella 19
20124 Milan
www.cai.it

Liechtenstein Alpine Club (Liechtensteiner Alpenverein, LAV)
Steinegerta 26
9494 Schaan
www.alpenverein.li

Slovenian Alpine Association (Planinska zveza Slovenije, PZS)
Dvorakova 9
p. p. 214
1001 Ljubljana
www.en.pzs.si

South Tyrol Alpine Club (Alpenverein Südtirol, AVS)
Giottostr. 3
39100 Bozen
www.alpenverein.it

Swiss Alpine Club (Schweizer Alpen-Club, SAC; Club Alpin Suisse, CAS; Club Alpino Svizzero, CAS; Club Alpin Svizzer, CAS)
Monbijoustr. 61
Postfach
3000 Bern 14
www.sac-cas.ch

Map suppliers
Cordee
www.cordee.co.uk

Stanfords
12–14 Long Acre
London
WC2E 9LP
www.stanfords.co.uk

The Map Shop
15 High Street
Upton-upon-Severn
WR8 0HJ
www.themapshop.co.uk

Resources for walking and trekking in the Alps

Austrian Alpine Club (UK Branch)
See above for contact details.
Benefits of AAC (UK) membership include:
• automatic worldwide mountain rescue and repatriation insurance

- reduced costs for accommodation in most alpine huts
- hut-to-hut tours
- grants for training courses in the Alps and UK
- organised meets in the Alps and other European ranges.

British Association of International Mountain Leaders
Siabod Cottage
Capel Curig
Conwy
LL24 0ES
www.baiml.org

The BAIML represents qualified trekking guides working abroad.

British Mountaineering Council
See above for contact details.
Although the BMC's main focus is to represent the interests of climbers, hill walkers and mountaineers by helping to maintain access to hill, crag and mountain areas in the UK, in partnership with the Association of Mountaineering Instructors it also offers subsidised courses for a range of activities, including walking and winter trekking. Insurance cover for mountain-based activities at home and abroad can also be arranged through the BMC.

Touching Nature
www.touchingnature.co.uk
A very useful online planning resource for mountain walking and hutting in the Alps.

Tourist information (alpine countries)
Austrian National Tourist Office
9–11 Richmond Buildings
London
W1D 3HF
www.austria.info/uk

French Government Tourist Office
178 Piccadilly
London
W1J 9AL
http://uk.france.fr

Italian State Tourist Board
1 Princes Street
London
W1B 2AY
www.italiantouristboard.co.uk

Slovenian Tourist Office
10 Little College Street
London
SW1P 3SH
www.slovenia.info

Switzerland Travel Centre
30 Bedford Street
London
WC2E 9ED
www.switzerlandtravelcentre.co.uk

Trekking and hut-to-hut holidays in the Alps
Alpine Exploratory
www.alpineexploratory.com
Guided and self-guided treks and hut tours

Alpine Treks
www.alpinetreks.co.uk
Guided and self-guided treks and hut tours

Exodus Travels
www.exodus.co.uk
Guided trekking holidays

Collett's Mountain Holidays
www.colletts.co.uk
Self-guided hut-to-hut tours in Austria and the Dolomites

Mountain Kingdoms
www.mountainkingdoms.com
Guided treks in the Alps and elsewhere

Sherpa Expeditions
www.sherpaexpeditions.com
Guided and self-guided treks in the Alps

Trekking in the Alps
www.trekkinginthealps.com
Guided summer trekking and winter snowshoeing holidays in the Alps

APPENDIX B
Directory of alpine huts

There are many hundreds of mountain huts, *gîtes d'étape* and *Berghotels* around the European Alps. It is beyond our scope to include them all here, so this list is limited to those that are featured in this book.

Refuge **Albert Premier** (1er)	www.refugealbert1er.ffcam.fr	Mont Blanc range, France
Berghotel **Almagelleralp**	www.almagelleralp.ch	Pennine Alps, Switzerland
Refuge de l'**Alpe de Villar d'Arène**	http://refugealpedevillardarene.ffcam.fr	Massif des Écrins, Dauphiné Alps, France
Rifugio **Alpe di Tires**	www.tierseralp.com	Dolomites, Italy
Alpenhof Stechelberg	www.alpenhof-stechelberg.ch	Bernese Alps, Switzerland
Berghaus **Alpiglen**	www.alpiglen.ch	Bernese Alps, Switzerland
Anton-Karg-Haus (Hinterbärenbad)	www.hinterbaerenbad.at	Kaisergebirge, Austria
Cabane d'**Arpitettaz**	www.arpitettaz.ch	Pennine Alps, Switzerland
Refuge de l'**Arpont**	www.refuges-vanoise.com	Graian Alps, France
Rifugio **Auronzo**	www.rifugioauronzo.it	Dolomites, Italy
Refuge de la **Balme**	www.refuge-balme-tarentaise.fr	Mont Blanc range, France
Refuge des **Bans**	www.refugedesbans.ffcam.fr	Massif des Écrins, Dauphiné Alps, France
Berghaus **Bäregg**	www.baeregg.com	Bernese Alps, Switzerland
Refuge de la **Barmaz**	www.gym-mache.ch	Pennine Alps, Switzerland
Refuge de **Bellachat**	www.refugebellachat.com	Mont Blanc range, France
Berliner Hut	www.berlinerhuette.at	Zillertal Alps, Austria
Rifugio **Bertone**	www.rifugiobertone.it	Mont Blanc range, Italy
Rifugio **Bignami**	www.rifugiobignami.it	Bernina Alps, Italy
Rifugio **Boè**	www.rifugioboe.it/home.htm	Dolomites, Italy
Rifugio **Bolzano**/Schlernhaus	www.schlernhaus.it	Dolomites, Italy
Rifugio **Bonatti**	www.rifugiobonatti.it	Mont Blanc range, Italy
Chalet de **Bonneval sur Arc**	www.chaletbonnevalsurarc.ffcam.fr	Graian Alps, France
Bordier Hut	www.bordierhuette.ch	Pennine Alps, Switzerland
Boval Hut (Chamanna Boval)	www.boval.ch	Bernina Alps, Switzerland
Rifugio **Boz**	www.caifeltre.it	Dolomites, Italy
Braunschweiger Hut	www.braunschweiger-huette.at	Ötztal Alps, Austria
Bremer Hut	www.bremerhuette.at	Stubai Alps, Austria
Cabane **Brunet**	www.cabanebrunet.ch	Pennine Alps, Switzerland
Burg Hut	www.burghuette.ch	Bernese Alps, Switzerland
Rifugio **Carate Brianza**	www.rifugiocarate.it	Bernina Alps, Italy
Carschina Hut	www.carschina.ch	Rätikon Alps, Switzerland
Rifugio **Castiglioni**	www.rifugiomarmolada.it	Dolomites, Italy
Rifugio **Cavaglia**	www.rifugiocavaglia.ch	Bernina Alps, Italy
Cabane de **Chanrion**	www.chanrion.ch	Pennine Alps, Switzerland
Rifugio **Città di Bressanone**/ Plosehütte	www.plosehuette.com	Dolomites, Italy
Refuge du **Clot**	www.refuge-clot.csvss.fr	Massif des Écrins, Dauphiné Alps, France
Cluozza Hut (Chamanna Cluozza)	www.nationalpark.ch	Bernina Alps, Switzerland
Coaz Hut (Chamanna Coaz)	www.coaz.ch/en	Bernina Alps, Switzerland
Refuge du **Col de Balme**	www.autourdumontblanc.com	Mont Blanc range, Switzerland

Refuge du **Col de la Vanoise**/		
Félix Faure	www.refugecoldelavanoise.ffcam.fr	Graian Alps, France
Cabane du **Combal**	www.autourdumontblanc.com	Mont Blanc range, Italy
Refuge du **Couvercle**	https://refugeducouvercle.jimdo.com	Mont Blanc range, France
Refuge de la **Croix du Bonhomme**	www.refugecroixdubonhomme.ffcam.fr	Mont Blanc range, France
Berghaus **Diavolezza**	www.diavolezza.ch	Bernina Alps, Switzerland
Cabane des **Dix**	www.cabanedesdix.ch	Pennine Alps, Switzerland
Douglass Hut	www.douglasshuette.at	Rätikon Alps, Austria
Drei Zinnen Hut/Rifugio Locatelli	www.dreizinnenhuette.com	Dolomites, Italy
Dresdner Hut	www.dresdnerhuette.at	Stubai Alps, Austria
Cabane des **Ecoulaies**	www.lespyramides.ch	Pennine Alps, Switzerland
Rifugio **Elena**	www.rifugioelena.it	Mont Blanc range, Italy
Rifugio **Elisabetta**	www.rifugioelisabetta.com	Mont Blanc range, Italy
Refuge **Entre Deux Eaux**	www.refugeentredeuxeaux.com	Graian Alps, France
Erzherzog-Johann Hut	www.erzherzog-johann-huette.at	Glockner Group, Austria
Capanna **Fassa**	www.rifugiocapannapizfassa.com	Dolomites, Italy
Berghotel **Faulhorn**	www.berghotel-faulhorn.ch	Bernese Alps, Switzerland
Refuge **Félix Faure**/		
du Col de la Vanoise	www.refugecoldelavanoise.ffcam.fr	Graian Alps, France
Refuge de la **Femma**	www.refugelafemma.com	Graian Alps, France
Rifugio **Firenze**/Regensburgerhütte	www.rifugiofirenze.com	Dolomites, Italy
Berggasthaus **First**	www.berggasthausfirst.ch	Bernese Alps, Switzerland
Refuge de la **Flégère**	www.autourdumontblanc.com	Mont Blanc range, France
Franz Senn Hut	www.franzsennhuette.at	Stubai Alps, Austria
Rifugio **Fredarola**	www.fredarola.it	Dolomites, Italy
Gafadura Hut	www.gafadurahuette.li	Rätikon Alps, Liechtenstein
Alpengasthof Gamperdona	www.himmelwirt.com	Rätikon Alps, Austria
Gaudeamus Hut	www.dav-main-spessart.de	Kaisergebirge, Austria
Refugio **Genova**/Schlüterhütte	www.schlueterhuette.com	Dolomites, Italy
Georgy Hut	www.georgy-huette.ch	Bernina Alps, Switzerland
Bivacco **Gervasutti**	www.sucai.it/bivaccogervasutti	Mont Blanc range, Italy
Gleckstein Hut	www.gleckstein.ch	Bernese Alps, Switzerland
Gletscherstube Märjela	www.gletscherstube.ch	Bernese Alps, Switzerland
Refuge du **Goûter**	www.refugedugouter.ffcam.fr	Mont Blanc range, France
Refuge des **Grands Mulets**	www.refugedesgrandsmulets.ffcam.fr	Mont Blanc range, France
Griesner Alm	www.griesneralm.at	Kaisergebirge, Austria
Berghaus **Grindelwaldblick**	www.grindelwaldblick.ch	Bernese Alps, Switzerland
Grutten Hut	www.grutten-huette.at	Kaisergebirge, Austria
Heinrich Hueter Hut	www.hueterhuette.at	Rätikon Alps, Austria
Hinterbärenbad (Anton-Karg-Haus)	www.hinterbaerenbad.at	Kaisergebirge, Austria
Hofer Alpl	www.hoferalpl.it	Dolomites, Italy
Innsbrucker Hut	www.innsbrucker-huette.at	Stubai Alps, Austria
Jamtal Hut	www.jamtalhuette.at	Silvretta Alps, Austria
Refuge du **Lac Blanc**	www.refugedulacblanc.fr	Mont Blanc range, France
Rifugio **Lagazuoi**	www.rifugiolagazuoi.com	Dolomites, Italy
Rifugio **Lago Palù**	www.rifugiopalu.it	Bernina Alps, Italy
Lauteraar Hut	www.sac-zofingen.ch	Bernese Alps, Switzerland
Rifugio **Lavaredo**	www.rifugiolavaredo.com	Dolomites, Italy

Gîte **Le Béranger**	www.gite-leberanger.fr	Massif des Écrins, Dauphiné Alps, France
Refuge de la **Leisse**	www.refugedelaleisse-vanoise.com	Graian Alps, France
Lindauer Hut	www.lindauerhuette.at	Rätikon Alps, Austria
Rifugio **Locatelli**/Drei Zinnen Hut	www.dreizinnenhuette.com	Dolomites, Italy
Rifugio **Longoni**	www.rifugi.lombardia.it	Bernina Alps, Italy
Cabane de **Louvie**	www.louvie.ch	Pennine Alps, Switzerland
Rifugio **Maison Vieille**	www.maisonvieille.com	Mont Blanc range, Italy
Berghaus **Männdlenen**	www.berghaus-maenndlenen.ch	Bernese Alps, Switzerland
Mannheimer Hut	www.dav-mannheim.de/huetten	Rätikon Alps, Switzerland
Capanna **Margherita**	www.rifugimonterosa.it	Pennine Alps, Italy
Rifugio **Marinelli Bombardieri**	www.rifugiomarinellibombardieri.it	Bernina Alps, Italy
Hôtel de **Mauvoisin**	www.hoteldemauvoisin.ch	Pennine Alps, Switzerland
Refuge de **Miage**	www.refugedemiage.com	Mont Blanc range, France
Cabane de **Mille**	www.cabanedemille.ch	Pennine Alps, Switzerland
Albergo **Miralago**	www.albergomiralago.com	Dolomites, Italy
Refuge de **Moëde-Anterne**	www.refuge-moede-anterne.com	Chablais Alps, France
Cabane de **Moiry**	www.cabane-de-moiry.ch	Pennine Alps, Switzerland
Monte Rosa Hut	www.section-monte-rosa.ch	Pennine Alps, Switzerland
Cabane du **Mont-Fort**	www.cabanemontfort.ch	Pennine Alps, Switzerland
Refuge des **Mottets**	www.lesmottets.com	Mont Blanc range, France
Cabane du **Mountet**	www.cas-diablerets.ch	Pennine Alps, Switzerland
Rifugio **Mulaz** (Volpi al Mulaz)	www.caiveneto.it/rifugi	Dolomites, Italy
Refuge de la **Muzelle**	www.muzelle.a-venosc.com	Massif des Écrins, Dauphiné Alps, France
Neue Regensburger Hut	www.regensburgerhuette.at	Stubai Alps, Austria
Nürnberger Hut	www.nuernbergerhuette.at	Stubai Alps, Austria
Berghotel **Obersteinberg**	www.stechelberg.ch	Bernese Alps, Switzerland
Refuge de l'**Orgère**	www.refuges-vanoise.com	Graian Alps, France
Cabane de **Panossière**	www.cabane-fxb-panossiere.ch/en	Pennine Alps, Switzerland
Rifugio **Passo Cereda**	www.passocereda.eu	Dolomites, Italy
Rifugio **Passo di Vizze**/ Pfitscherjoch-Haus	www.pfitscherjochhaus.com	Zillertal Alps, Italy
Rifugio **Passo Valles**	www.passovalles.com	Dolomites, Italy
Refuge de **Péclet-Polset**	www.refugepecletpolset.ffcam.fr	Graian Alps, France
Peter Tscherrig Anen Hut	www.anenhuette.ch	Bernese Alps, Switzerland
Cabane du **Petit Mountet**	www.petitmountet.ch	Pennine Alps, Switzerland
Pfälzer Hut Pfitscherjoch-Haus/	www.alpenverein.li	Rätikon Alps, Liechtenstein
Rifugio Passo di Vizze	www.pfitscherjochhaus.com	Zillertal Alps, Italy
Rifugio dal **Piaz**	www.rifugiodalpiaz.com	Dolomites, Italy
Rifugio **Pisciadù**	www.rifugiopisciadu.it	Dolomites, Italy
Refuge du **Plan du Lac**	www.refugeplandulac.com	Graian Alps, France
Refuge de **Plan Sec**	www.refuges-vanoise.com	Graian Alps, France
Rifugio **Pradidali**	www.rifugiopradidali.com	Dolomites, Italy
Refuge du **Pré de la Chaumette**	www.refugepredelachaumette.ffcam.fr	Massif des Écrins, Dauphiné Alps, France
Rifugio **Puez**	www.rifugiopuez.it	Dolomites, Italy

The Mountain Hut Book

Regensburgerhütte/Rifugio Firenze	www.rifugiofirenze.com	Dolomites, Italy
Riedl Hut	www.riedlhuette.at	Kaisergebirge, Austria
Rinder Hut	www.torrent.ch	Bernese Alps, Switzerland
Hotel Roseggletscher	www.roseg-gletscher.ch	Bernina Alps, Switzerland
Rifugio Rosetta	www.rifugiorosetta.it	Dolomites, Italy
Rothorn Hut	www.sac-oberaargau.ch	Pennine Alps, Switzerland
Rotstock Hut	www.rotstockhuette.ch	Bernese Alps, Switzerland
Rottal Hut	www.sac-interlaken.ch	Bernese Alps, Switzerland
Schesaplana Hut	www.schesaplana-huette.ch	Rätikon Alps, Switzerland
Schlernhaus/Rifugio Bolzano	www.schlernhaus.it	Dolomites, Italy
Schlüterhütte/Refugio Genova	www.schlueterhuette.com	Dolomites, Italy
Hotel Schynige Platte	www.hotelschynigeplatte.ch	Bernese Alps, Switzerland
Refuge du Sélé	www.refugedusele.ffcam.fr	Massif des Écrins, Dauphiné Alps, France
Refuge de la Selle	www.refugedelaselle.fr	Massif des Écrins, Dauphiné Alps, France
Pension Sonnenberg	www.sonnenberg-muerren.ch	Bernese Alps, Switzerland
Refuge des Souffles	www.refugedessouffles.ffcam.fr	Massif des Écrins, Dauphiné Alps, France
Starkenburger Hut	www.alpenverein-darmstadt.de	Stubai Alps, Austria
Stripsenjochhaus	www.stripsenjoch.at	Kaisergebirge, Austria
Suls-Lobhorn Hut	www.lobhornhuette.ch	Bernese Alps, Switzerland
Sulzenau Hut	www.sulzenauhuette.at	Stubai Alps, Austria
Pension Suppenalp	www.suppenalp.ch	Bernese Alps, Switzerland
Rifugio del Teodulo	www.rifugioteodulo.com	Pennine Alps, Italy
Tilisuna Hut	www.alpenverein.at	Rätikon Alps, Austria
Totalp Hut	www.totalp.at	Rätikon Alps, Austria
Cabane de Tracuit	www.tracuit.ch	Pennine Alps, Switzerland
Rifugio Treviso	www.rifugiotreviso.it	Dolomites, Italy
Triglav Hut/		
Triglavski dom na Kredarici	www.en.pzs.si	Julian Alps, Slovenia
Berggasthaus Tschingelhorn	www.tschingelhorn.ch	Bernese Alps, Switzerland
Refuge de Vallonbrun	www.refuge-vallonbrun.com	Graian Alps, France
Refuge de Vallonpierre	www.vallonpierre.com	Massif des Écrins, Dauphiné Alps, France
Berghaus Vereina	www.berghausvereina.ch	Silvretta Alps, Switzerland
Rifugio Viel dal Pan	www.rifugiovieldalpan.com	Dolomites, Italy
Cabane des Vignettes	www.cabanedesvignettes.ch	Pennine Alps, Switzerland
Rifugio Vittorio Sella	www.rifugiosella.com	Gran Paradiso National Park, Italy
Vorderkaiserfelden Hut	www.vorderkaiserfelden.com	Kaisergebirge, Austria
Warnsdorfer Hut	www.warnsdorferhuette.at	Venediger Group, Austria
Hotel Wetterhorn	www.hotelwetterhorn.ch	Bernese Alps, Switzerland

APPENDIX C
Glossary for alpine trekkers

French	English
aiguille	needle-like peak
arête	ridge – see also crête
auberge	simple inn
bière	beer
boisson	drink
cabane	mountain hut – see also refuge
carte de randonnée	map showing walking routes
cirque	steep three-sided valley headwall or amphitheatre
couloir	gully
crête	ridge – see also arête
déjeuner	lunch
dîner	evening meal/dinner
dortoir	dormitory
eau (non) potable	water (not) suitable for drinking
gardien(ne)	hut warden (male/female)
gîte d'étape	walkers' hostel
glace	ice
mauvais pas	bad step or difficult place
névé	snowfield that feeds a glacier (G. Firn)
petit déjeuner	breakfast
plan	plateau or plain
refuge	mountain hut – see also cabane
repas	meal
sac à dos	rucksack
sac à viande	sheet sleeping bag
sac de couchage	sleeping bag
sentier	path
source	spring (water)
téléphérique	cable car
télésiège	chairlift

German	English
Abendessen	evening meal/dinner
Alp/Alpe/Alm	summer farm or pasture, usually above the treeline
Alpenverein	alpine club
Aussichtspunkt	viewpoint
Bergsteiger	mountaineer
Bergsteigeressen	mountaineer's low-cost meal
Bergweg	mountain path
Biwak	a simple unmanned mountain hut (It. bivacco)
Fels	rock
Firn	snowfield that feeds a glacier (Fr. névé)
Frühstück	breakfast
Gletscher	glacier
Grat	ridge
Höhenweg	high route (It. alta via)
Hütte	mountain hut
Hüttenwirt	hut warden
Joch	mountain pass or saddle
Klettersteig	protected way or aided climbing route (It. via ferrata)
Kopf	peak
Lawine	avalanche
Massenlager	dormitory – also Matratzenlager, literally a 'mattress room'
Materialseilbahn	mountain hut's goods lift
Mittagessen	lunch
Moräne	moraine
nur für Geübte	only for those with experience
Scharte	narrow pass
Schlucht	gorge
Seilbahn	cable car
Stausee	reservoir
Steinschlag	rockfall
Stube	common room
Tagessuppe	soup of the day
Touristenlager	dormitory – see also Massenlager
Trockenraum	drying room
Wanderkarte	walkers' map
Wanderweg	footpath
Winterraum	a hut's winter room (It. ricovero invernale)
Zeltplatz	campsite

Italian	English
acqua (non) potabile	water (not) suitable for drinking
albergo	hotel
alta via	high route (G. Höhenweg)
altopiano	high-altitude plateau
baita	alpine farm
bivacco	unmanned mountain hut (G. Biwak)
bocca/bocchetta	mountain pass – see also forcella
campeggio	campsite
capanna	mountain refuge – see also chamanna (Rom.) and rifugio
carta dei sentieri	walkers' map
chamanna	mountain hut (Rom.) – see also capanna and rifugio
cima	summit or peak
cresta	ridge
dormitorio	dormitory
forcella	mountain pass – see also bocca and bocchetta
funivia	cable car
gestore del rifugio	hut keeper or warden
ghiaccio	glacier – see also vedretta
malga	alp or high mountain farm
passo	mountain pass – see also porta
pericolo	danger
porta	mountain pass – see also passo
posto tappa	walkers' hostel
ricovero invernale	winter room (G. Winterraum)
rifugio	mountain hut – see also capanna and chamanna (Rom.)
seggiovia	chairlift
sentiero	path or route
teleferica	mountain hut's goods lift (G. Materialseilbahn)
vedretta	glacier – see also ghiaccio
via ferrata	protected path, literally 'iron way' (G. Klettersteig)

Slovene	English
apartma	apartment
čaj	tea
dober dan	hello
dolina	valley
dom/koča	mountain hut
góra	mountain
gostílna	inn
grebén	ridge
jézero	lake
kava	coffee
kosílo	lunch
ledeník	glacier
nahrbtnik	rucksack
planina	alp pasture
póstelja	bed
pot	path – see also stezá
sedlo	saddle, or pass
skúpno lezisče	dormitory
sneg	snow
sóba	room
stezá	path – see also pot
voda	water
vrh	summit
zájtrk	breakfast

Other terms	
alp	summer farm or pasture, usually above the treeline
col	mountain pass or saddle
combe	mountain basin, like a cirque but usually more gently formed
trek	multi-day journey on foot

APPENDIX D
Further reading

The mountaineering library is vast. Volumes which deal with the Alps run into the thousands, so the following list is very selective: it is limited to a few of those titles which either deal with the development of mountaineering in the Alps or contain items regarding the siting, creation or use of mountain huts. A number of these are out of print, but copies may be available through the public library system, or obtainable through specialist book websites.

Adam Smith, Janet: *Mountain Holidays* (Dent, 1946)
A writer feted for her elegant prose, Janet Adam Smith (1905–99) was also known for her great love of mountains and mountaineering. She and her husband, the climber and poet Michael Roberts, made a number of visits to the Alps from the 1920s on, and after becoming a widow in 1948 she returned to climb such classic routes as the Mer de Glace face of the Grépon and the traverse of the Meije. As these were achieved long after *Mountain Holidays* was written, they are not mentioned in this memoir, in which she admits that her aim was not to establish records but simply to enjoy herself. As a result, her book celebrates that sense of joyous freedom which draws so many of us back to the mountains year after year, and is full of perceptive descriptions. The Dolomites, she says, are 'shocks and freaks of crude pink stone, whose shape, proportion, and colour bear no relation to the valleys from which they spring.' On the pleasures of summiting the Rimpfischhorn, she writes of: 'that utter satisfaction of the top reached, the day fine, the body satisfied, and the glories of the world for the eye to look at.' And when it comes to huts, she conjures up the difficulties of killing time when trapped for days by storm: 'We slept, looked through the visitors' book, gossiped, ate, looked at maps, practised knots with spare bootlaces, slept, argued about God, and washed shirts which froze stiff...'; and she described the Victor Emmanuel hut below the Gran Paradiso as 'a gigantic aluminium dog-kennel'. As well as her own books, Janet Adam Smith translated a number of French mountaineering classics into English, most notably Maurice Herzog's *Annapurna*.

Barry, John: *Alpine Climbing* (Crowood Press, 1988)
The subtitle says it all, for this is *The Handbook of Alpine Climbing*, in effect an updated version of Part 3 of Alan Blackshaw's influential *Mountaineering*. It is a comprehensive 'how to' manual written with the author's hallmark light touch, with humour as the leaven to some serious business. In a section on huts and refuges, he refers to the 'usual sleeping arrangements [as] room-wide bunks with ten or more to a bunk – commingling heat!' John Barry (b. 1944) is an experienced climber, writer and raconteur, a one-time Royal Marine and former Director of the National Mountain Centre at Plas y Brenin, with numerous major ascents to his credit in ranges as far apart as Alaska, New Zealand, the Alps, Norway, the Karakoram and the Himalaya.

Bonington, Chris: *Mountaineer* (Diadem, 1989)
A large-format pictorial account of the life and climbs of Britain's mountaineering 'ambassador'.

Braham, Trevor: *When the Alps Cast Their Spell* (The In Pinn, 2004)
Many books have been written about the 'golden age' of alpine mountaineering, but few can match this scholarly yet eminently readable retelling of some of the best-known stories of climbs and pass crossings through the portraits of those who took a leading role in them. In writing this book, Braham, a prominent figure in the mountaineering world (he made his first visit to the Alps in 1948 and was one-time editor of the *Himalayan Journal*), had the aim of bringing to life 'the atmosphere of those far-off days, when every venture aroused a sense of wonder.' And this he does admirably.

Buhl, Hermann: *Nanga Parbat Pilgrimage* (Hodder & Stoughton, 1956; latest edition, Bâton Wicks, 1998)
Remembered for his bold ascent in 1953 of Himalayan giant Nanga Parbat, Austrian mountaineer Hermann Buhl (1924–57) learned his craft among the Eastern Alps before, during and after World War II.

He made countless difficult climbs in winter and in summer, many of them solo ascents recalled in this book, which inspired a whole generation of climbers. Buhl was a frequent user of Austria's huts, and the book includes mention of several of them.

Clark, Ronald W: *The Alps* (Weidenfeld & Nicolson, 1973); *The Early Alpine Guides* (Phoenix House, 1949); *Men, Myths & Mountains* (Weidenfeld & Nicolson, 1976); *A Picture History of Mountaineering* (Hulton Press, 1956); *The Victorian Mountaineers* (Batsford, 1953)
A prolific and distinguished biographer and author of both fiction and non-fiction books, Ronald Clark (1916–87) wrote widely on mountaineering history, of which he was an acknowledged expert. All the above titles contain much of interest to anyone studying the exploration of the Alps.

Conway, WM: *The Alps from End to End* (Constable, 1895)
In 1894, William Martin Conway (1856–1937) set out to make the first end-to-end traverse of the Alps. Often quoted as being from Monte Viso to the Grossglockner, it actually began in Italy at the foot of the Col de Tende (about 40km from the Mediterranean) and ended 87 days later on the summit of Ankogel east of the Grossglockner near Salzburg in Austria. While others (termed 'centrists') concentrated on the ascent of specific peaks from a single base, Conway was a leading 'ex-centrist' – a man who loved to make journeys across the mountains. Apart from to the Alps, this also led him to Spitsbergen, the Andes and the Karakoram. During his end-to-end trek, Conway was able to record his impressions of some of the earliest of mountain huts established by the Alpine Clubs, and to contrast them with a few of the flea-ridden inns and so-called hotels that remained in remote villages as a reminder of the Dark Ages. Nearly 120 years after Conway made that epic journey across the Alps, Simon Thompson set out to follow in his footsteps; and in *A Long Walk with Lord Conway* (see below), he not only compares the Alps then and now, but also reveals a more complex side to Conway's character than the one he liked to portray of himself.

Dumler, Helmut and Burkhardt, Willi P: *The High Mountains of the Alps* (Diadem, 1994)
Translated from the German by Tim Carruthers and adapted by publisher Ken Wilson from the original *Die Viertausender der Alpen*, this large-format, beautifully illustrated book not only gives a brief history of climbing all the alpine 4000m peaks but also outlines some of the major routes created on them since their first ascent. A summary at the end of each chapter includes a note about the huts used on the various routes for specific peaks. It is a volume that not only inspires dreams among all who love the Alps but also provides some of the clues to making them come true.

Fedden, Robin: *The Enchanted Mountains: A Quest in the Pyrenees* (John Murray, 1962)
A minor classic, this is an unashamedly romantic tale of mountaineering in the Pyrenees in the 1950s. Robin Fedden (1908–77) was a one-time diplomat who only turned to mountaineering in his thirties, but made up for lost time with activity in the mountains of Turkey, Greece, Peru, the Alps and the Indian Himalaya. The three Pyrenean seasons that form the substance of *The Enchanted Mountains* seem now like a lost age.

Frison-Roche, Roger: *Mont Blanc and the Seven Valleys* (Nicholas Kaye, 1961)
In this book, mountain guide and writer Frison-Roche (1906–99) describes the Mont Blanc massif, its valleys and the culture of its villages in a logical 'Tour of Mont Blanc' journey, illustrated with more than 150 full-page black-and-white photographs by Pierre Tairraz.

Irving, RLG: *The Alps* (Batsford, 1939)
Winchester schoolmaster and mountaineer Robert Lock Graham Irving (1877–1969) was the man who introduced Mallory to climbing. An alpine connoisseur who wrote a number of books, this title covers almost the whole range in eloquent prose.

Kennedy, ES: 'Ascent of the Pizzo Bernina', in ES Kennedy (ed.) *Peaks, Passes and Glaciers: Being Excursions by Members of the Alpine Club*, second series, vol. 1 (Longman, Green, Longman, and Roberts, 1862)

Edward Shirley Kennedy (1817–98) was one of those wealthy Victorians who developed a passion for the Alps when there were still many high peaks left to climb. He was one of the founding fathers of the Alpine Club, its president (1860–62), and editor of the second series of *Peaks, Passes and Glaciers* in 1862.

Klucker, Christian: *Adventures of an Alpine Guide* (John Murray, 1932)
Originally published in Germany shortly after his death in 1928, this autobiography of a well-respected guide of mountaineering's 'silver age' tells of his relationship with various mountaineers of the late 1800s, as well as recounting some of his most famous climbs. But the book is also of interest with regard to the provision and siting of a number of huts in south-east Switzerland, for which he had responsibility. Born in 1853 in the Engadine offshoot of Val Fex, Klucker was one of the foremost guides of his time, equally at home on rock and ice, with a great gift for discovering new routes for his employers. In a long and illustrious career (he climbed until the year before his death at the age of 75), he made numerous new climbs, traverses and ascents ranging from the Dolomites to the Dauphiné Alps, took part in the first traverse of the Peuterey Ridge in 1893, and in 1901 went to Canada with Whymper.

Le Vay, David: *A Tour of Mont Blanc* (Summersdale, 2014)
A light-hearted personal account of walking one of the world's most popular treks.

Levi, Primo: 'Bear Meat', *The New Yorker* (8 January 2007)
In this short story, Italian chemist, writer and Holocaust survivor Primo Levi (1919–87) relates climbers' tales during a stay in a mountain hut.

Lieberman, Marcia R: *Walking Switzerland the Swiss Way* (Cordee, 1987)
American author Marcia Lieberman has produced several guides to walking in the Alps. In *Walking Switzerland the Swiss Way* she introduces her readers to a variety of accommodation options when tackling walks from five different resorts.

Maeder, Herbert: *The Mountains of Switzerland* (George Allen & Unwin, 1968)
A large-format book of excellent full-page black-and-white photographs, complemented by essays that provide an overall portrait of the Swiss Alps.

Milner, C Douglas: *The Dolomites* (Robert Hale, 1951)
Milner's love of the Dolomites runs throughout this book as he journeys through each district with the eye of a climber roaming from one romantic scene to the next. As with his Mont Blanc, his tour of the Dolomites is spattered with worthwhile quotes.

Milner, C Douglas: *Mont Blanc and the Aiguilles* (Robert Hale, 1955)
A well-known member of the Alpine Club, Douglas Milner wrote and illustrated several books about mountains, climbing and photography. In *Mont Blanc and the Aiguilles*, he introduces his readers to individual parts of the massif and tells their mountaineering history.

Moore, AW: *The Alps in 1864* (privately published, 1867; Blackwell edition, 1939)
Published in two volumes, Moore's book provides a vivid account of mountaineering's 'golden age', in which he played an active part. In 1864 he made six first ascents of major peaks or cols in the Alps, as well as several second or third ascents, while in 1865 he claimed first ascents of Piz Roseg, the Obergabelhorn and the Brenva Face of Mont Blanc. A number of his climbs were made with Whymper, and it is interesting to compare Moore's account of some of their shared adventures with those recorded in Whymper's *Scrambles*. Beyond the Alps, he visited the Caucasus in 1868 when he made the first ascent of Mount Kazbek with Freshfield, Tuckett and their guide, François Devouassoud, and reached the East Summit of Mount Elbrus. Apart from his mountaineering career, Adolphus Warburton Moore (1841–87) served for a time as private secretary to Lord Randolph Churchill, and was a senior official in the India Office.

Pilley, Dorothy: *Climbing Days* (Bell & Sons, 1935)
In this autobiographical record of her climbs between the two World Wars, we gain an insight into the way huts were then used. The author's first 'proper' alpine refuge was the Couvercle; at the time of her visit (1920) this was just a tiny overcrowded hut tucked below an overhanging slab of granite, but despite the unaccustomed privations she endured there, she soon became a keen advocate of huts in general and her book is peppered with descriptions and incidents connected with staying in them – not just in the Alps, but also in the Pyrenees. Dorothy Pilley (1894–1986) was one of the most influential women mountaineers of the early 20th century. Married to the literary academic and fellow climber IA Richards, she climbed extensively in the Alps in the 1920s, and further afield after that. She served as secretary of the Ladies Alpine Club and president of the Pinnacle Club, and at the age of 91, in the bitter cold January of 1986, she travelled to Skye with a nephew and spent a night at the Glen Brittle Hut, drinking whisky and recounting mountain stories to a group of young climbers also staying there.

Richards, Dan: *Climbing Days* (Faber & Faber, 2016)
A little over 80 years after Dorothy Pilley's Climbing Days was published, a second, highly entertaining book with the same title appeared. The author, Dan Richards, is descended from Dorothy Pilley, and in creating a portrait of the great-great-aunt he never met, he follows her to Snowdonia, the Lake District and the Cairngorms. Retracing her footsteps to the Alps, he meets a descendant of her favourite guide and a number of people who remember her with affection. He also climbs the Dent Blanche, which she'd climbed in 1928, and overnights in the Cabane de Bertol above Arolla, where she had first stayed in 1921. As late arrivals, he and his father prised off their boots and crept off to their dormitory, where he describes 'crawling over prone bodies in the blanket warmth, seeking empty berths with the aid of a muffled head torch, fully dressed, dog-tired...'. This is a delightful book in which the author describes his own adventures and misadventures in huts and on the mountains in a way that a number of alpine novices would relate to, but rarely confess.

Spring, Ira and Edwards, Harvey: *100 Hikes in the Alps* (Mountaineers Books, 1979)
The title says it all. Practically the whole range of the Alps (plus five routes in the Pyrenees) is covered, with black-and-white photographs by Ira Spring, and route descriptions and introduction by Harvey Edwards, including a section on huts.

Thompson, Simon: *A Long Walk with Lord Conway* (Signal Books, 2013)
Subtitled An *Exploration of the Alps and an English Adventurer,* this is a fascinating account of the author's retracing of WM Conway's *Alps from End to End* (see above). It departs from a standard mountain travelogue to become an intelligent unravelling of 'a charming rogue', previously feted as a distinguished art critic, explorer, mountaineer and writer. Simon Thompson is also the author of *Unjustifiable Risk? The Story of British Climbing* (Cicerone Press, 2010), and his flair for unearthing little-known details and retelling anecdotes makes his version of Conway's classic book a 'must-read' for anyone with an interest in the Alps as an evolving chain and the life of one of mountaineering's hitherto misinterpreted characters.

Unsworth, Walt: *Encyclopaedia of Mountaineering* (Hodder & Stoughton, 1975, 1977, 1992)
The third edition, compiled by noted mountain historian and founder of Cicerone Press, Walt Unsworth (1928–2017), makes a perfect reference tool for anyone interested in mountains and mountaineering.

Walker, J Hubert: *Walking in the Alps* (Oliver & Boyd, 1951)
Despite being out of date with regard to the size of villages, extent of glaciers and the depiction of numerous valleys, and in spite of being limited to the description of just nine districts, Walker's book remains one of the finest ever written about the Alps. Aimed at the walker and mountaineer 'of modest attainment' who was unfamiliar with the alpine range, Walker set out to describe the mountains and their valleys in orderly fashion, then outlined a plan for their discovery by suggesting tours that would lead from valley to valley across the passes, staying in huts and straying onto summits in a way that still excites six

decades on. His language is elegant, his hand-drawn maps precise in every detail, and the black-and-white photographs beautifully composed. Hubert Walker (1901–63) was born in the Lake District, was educated at Bath, became a geography teacher in Surrey, and visited the Alps at every opportunity. During World War II, he lectured on the Alps on behalf of the Council for Adult Education in HM Forces, and it was as a result of the eagerness of his 'students' that this book was written. Its practical relevance may be somewhat dated, but Walker's inspiration is timeless.

Whymper, Edward: *Scrambles Amongst the Alps* (John Murray, 1871; numerous editions since)
In July 1860, the young artist and engraver Edward Whymper went to the Alps for the first time to make some sketches on behalf of publisher William Longman, in order to illustrate *Peaks, Passes and Glaciers*, the forerunner of the Alpine Club's Alpine Journal. Until that summer, Whymper had never even set eyes upon a mountain, but five years later he was the first man to stand on the summit of the Matterhorn; it was to be the crowning glory of his life and the climax of the golden age of mountaineering. But by the time the sun went down that day, he had witnessed the death of four of his companions in a well-documented accident, and his own alpine career was all but over. Scrambles not only recounts the many attempts made by Whymper (1840–1911) before leading the first ascent of the Matterhorn, but also tells of the numerous climbs, pass crossings and lengthy journeys he made among the Alps during those momentous summers of 1860–65. Scrambles is one of the most famous of all adventure stories, and arguably the most influential mountaineering book of all time. As with the accounts of other mountaineers of the period, it tells us almost as much about the conditions endured by Whymper and his fellow climbers before making their ascents as it does about the ascents themselves.

Wills, Alfred: *Wanderings Among the High Alps* (Bentley, 1856; Blackwell edition, 1937)
This classic volume of memoirs provides an interesting view of the conditions in which alpine peasants lived in the 19th century, as well as describing the author's various journeys, pass crossings and climbs. His ascent of the Wetterhorn in 1854, although not the first, is usually accepted as ushering in the golden age of mountaineering, which ended with Whymper's tragic first ascent of the Matterhorn. Alfred Wills (1828–1912) was the son of a Justice of the Peace and a 'financially well-set-up fellow' whose adventures in the Alps were at odds with the comfortable lifestyle he and a number of his fellow Victorian pioneers enjoyed at home. During the course of his mountaineering and mountain travels, he stayed in some pretty dire hovels, which he describes (almost with relish) in his book. According to alpine historian Ronald Clark, he was the 'prototype of those gentlemen whose ordinary mountain wanderings developed into genuine mountain-climbing.' An original member of the Alpine Club, he was its president in 1864–65. In his professional life he was a barrister and a judge in the Queen's Bench Division, and is remembered as the man who tried Oscar Wilde.

Cicerone Press

Cicerone Press have produced a large number of practical guidebooks to hut-to-hut trekking and ski mountaineering in the Alps and elsewhere. The following list deals only with the Alps, but for titles covering mountain regions as diverse as those of the Pyrenees, Africa, Patagonia, the Himalaya, Iceland and Scandinavia, see www.cicerone.co.uk.

100 Hut Walks in the Alps
Across the Eastern Alps: E5
Alpine Ski Mountaineering – Vol 1: Western Alps
Alpine Ski Mountaineering – Vol 2: Central and Eastern Alps
Canyoning in the Alps
Chamonix Mountain Adventures
Chamonix to Zermatt: The Classic Walker's Haute Route
Ecrins National Park
Gran Paradiso
Innsbruck Mountain Adventures
Mont Blanc Walks
Mountain Adventures in the Maurienne
Mountain Biking in Slovenia
Shorter Walks in the Dolomites
Ski Touring and Snowshoeing in the Dolomites
Switzerland's Jura High Route
The Adlerweg
The Bernese Oberland
The GR5 Trail
The Julian Alps of Slovenia
The Karnischer Höhenweg
The Swiss Alpine Pass Route – Via Alpina 1
The Swiss Alps
Through the Italian Alps: The Grande Traversata delle Alpi
Tour of Mont Blanc
Tour of Monte Rosa
Tour of the Bernina
Tour of the Jungfrau Region
Tour of the Matterhorn
Tour of the Oisans: GR54
Tour of the Queyras
Tour of the Vanoise

Trail Running Chamonix
Trekking in Austria's Hohe Tauern
Trekking in Slovenia
Trekking in the Alps
Trekking in the Dolomites
Trekking in the Silvretta and Rätikon Alps
Trekking in the Stubai Alps
Trekking in the Zillertal Alps
Trekking Munich to Venice
Vanoise Ski Touring
Via Ferratas of the French Alps
Via Ferratas of the Italian Dolomites: Vol 1
Via Ferratas of the Italian Dolomites: Vol 2
Walking and Trekking in the Gran Paradiso
Walking in Austria
Walking in Italy's Stelvio National Park
Walking in Provence – East
Walking in Slovenia: The Karavanke
Walking in the Alps
Walking in the Bavarian Alps
Walking in the Briançonnais
Walking in the Dolomites
Walking in the Haute Savoie: North
Walking in the Haute Savoie: South
Walking in the Valais
Walking the Italian Lakes
Walks and Treks in the Maritime Alps
Walks in the Engadine – Switzerland

In addition, a number of Cicerone's alpine walking guides to specific regions include routes to huts and information about them. Mention should also be made of *The Book of the Bothy*, which concentrates on the unique chain of bothies found in the UK, and several books on techniques relevant to activities in the Alps.

INDEX

Index

The Mountain Hut Book

IF YOU ENJOYED THIS GUIDEBOOK
YOU MIGHT ALSO BE INTERESTED IN...

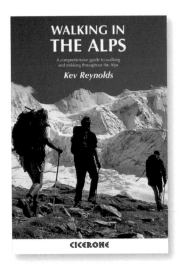

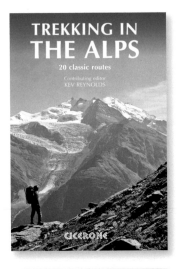

visit **www.cicerone.co.uk** for more detail
and our full range of guidebooks

LISTING OF CICERONE GUIDES

ITALY

Italy's Sibillini National Park
Shorter Walks in the Dolomites
Ski Touring and Snowshoeing in the Dolomites
The Way of St Francis
Through the Italian Alps
Trekking in the Apennines
Trekking in the Dolomites
Via Ferratas of the Italian Dolomites Volume 1
Via Ferratas of the Italian Dolomites: Vol 2
Walking and Trekking in the Gran Paradiso
Walking in Abruzzo
Walking in Italy's Stelvio National Park
Walking in Sardinia
Walking in Sicily
Walking in the Dolomites
Walking in Tuscany
Walking in Umbria
Walking on the Amalfi Coast
Walking the Italian Lakes
Walks and Treks in the Maritime Alps

SCANDINAVIA: NORWAY, SWEDEN, FINLAND

Walking in Norway

EASTERN EUROPE AND THE BALKANS

The Danube Cycleway Volume 2
The High Tatras
The Mountains of Romania
Walking in Bulgaria's National Parks
Walking in Hungary
Mountain Biking in Slovenia
The Islands of Croatia
The Julian Alps of Slovenia
The Mountains of Montenegro
The Peaks of the Balkans Trail
Trekking in Slovenia
Walking in Croatia
Walking in Slovenia: The Karavanke

SPAIN

Coastal Walks in Andalucia
Cycle Touring in Spain
Mountain Walking in Mallorca
Mountain Walking in Southern Catalunya
Spain's Sendero Histórico: The GR1
The Andalucian Coast to Coast Walk
The Mountains of Nerja
The Mountains of Ronda and Grazalema
The Northern Caminos
The Sierras of Extremadura

The Way of St James Cyclist Guide
Trekking in Mallorca
Walking and Trekking in the Sierra Nevada
Walking in Andalucia
Walking in Menorca
Walking in the Cordillera Cantabrica
Walking on Gran Canaria
Walking on La Gomera and El Hierro
Walking on La Palma
Walking on Lanzarote and Fuerteventura
Walking on Tenerife
Walking on the Costa Blanca

PORTUGAL

The Camino Portugués
Walking in Portugal
Walking in the Algarve

GREECE, CYPRUS AND MALTA

The High Mountains of Crete
Trekking in Greece
Walking and Trekking on Corfu
Walking in Cyprus
Walking on Malta

INTERNATIONAL CHALLENGES, COLLECTIONS AND ACTIVITIES

Canyoning in the Alps
The Via Francigena Canterbury to Rome – Parts 1 and 2

AFRICA

Climbing in the Moroccan Anti-Atlas
Mountaineering in the Moroccan High Atlas
The High Atlas
Trekking in the Atlas Mountains
Kilimanjaro
Walking in the Drakensberg

JORDAN

Jordan – Walks, Treks, Caves, Climbs and Canyons
Treks and Climbs in Wadi Rum, Jordan

ASIA

Annapurna
Everest: A Trekker's Guide
Trekking in the Himalaya
Trekking in Bhutan
Trekking in Ladakh
The Mount Kailash Trek

USA AND CANADA

British Columbia
The John Muir Trail
The Pacific Crest Trail

ARGENTINA, CHILE AND PERU

Aconcagua and the Southern Andes
Hiking and Biking Peru's Inca Trails
Torres del Paine

TECHNIQUES

Geocaching in the UK
Indoor Climbing
Lightweight Camping
Map and Compass
Outdoor Photography
Polar Exploration
Rock Climbing
Sport Climbing
The Mountain Hut Book

MINI GUIDES

Alpine Flowers
Avalanche!
Navigation
Pocket First Aid and Wilderness Medicine
Snow

MOUNTAIN LITERATURE

8000 metres
A Walk in the Clouds
Abode of the Gods
The Pennine Way – the Path, the People, the Journey
Unjustifiable Risk?

For full information on all our guides, books and eBooks,
visit our website:
www.cicerone.co.uk

Walking – Trekking – Mountaineering – Climbing – Cycling

Over 40 years, Cicerone have built up an outstanding collection of over 300 guides, inspiring all sorts of amazing adventures.

Every guide comes from extensive exploration and research by our expert authors, all with a passion for their subjects. They are frequently praised, endorsed and used by clubs, instructors and outdoor organisations.

All our titles can now be bought as **e-books**, **Epubs** and **Kindle** files and we also have an online magazine – **Cicerone Extra** – with features to help cyclists, climbers, walkers and trekkers choose their next adventure, at home or abroad.

Our website shows any **new information** we've had in since a book was published. Please do let us know if you find anything has changed, so that we can publish the latest details. On our **website** you'll also find great ideas and lots of detailed information about what's inside every guide and you can buy **individual routes** from many of them online.

It's easy to keep in touch with what's going on at Cicerone by getting our monthly **free e-newsletter**, which is full of offers, competitions, up-to-date information and topical articles. You can subscribe on our home page and also follow us on **Facebook** and **Twitter** or dip into our **blog**.

Cicerone – the very best guides for exploring the world.

ℂ𝕚ℂℰℝ𝕆ℕℰ

Juniper House, Murley Moss, Oxenholme Road, Kendal, Cumbria LA9 7RL

Tel: 015395 62069 info@cicerone.co.uk

www.cicerone.co.uk